OPPOSING VIEWPOINTS® SERIES

White-Collar Crime

Other Books of Related Interest:

"Congress shall make
no law . . . abridging
the freedom of speech,
or of the press."

First Amendment to the U.S. Constitution

The basic foundation of our democracy is the First Amendment guarantee of freedom of expression. The Opposing Viewpoints Series is dedicated to the concept of this basic freedom and the idea that it is more important to practice it than to enshrine it.

OPPOSING VIEWPOINTS® SERIES

White-Collar Crime

Kelly Wand, Book Editor

GREENHAVEN PRESS
A part of Gale, Cengage Learning

GALE
CENGAGE Learning™

Detroit • New York • San Francisco • New Haven, Conn • Waterville, Maine • London

GALE
CENGAGE Learning™

Christine Nasso, *Publisher*
Elizabeth Des Chenes, *Managing Editor*

© 2009 Greenhaven Press, a part of Gale, Cengage Learning.

Gale and Greenhaven Press are registered trademarks used herein under license.

For more information, contact:
Greenhaven Press
27500 Drake Rd.
Farmington Hills, MI 48331-3535
Or you can visit our Internet site at gale.cengage.com

For product information and technology assistance, contact us at

Gale Customer Support, 1-800-877-4253
For permission to use material from this text or product, submit all requests online at
www.cengage.com/permissions

Further permissions questions can be emailed to permissionrequest@cengage.com

Articles in Greenhaven Press anthologies are often edited for length to meet page require-ments. In addition, original titles of these works are changed to clearly present the main thesis and to explicitly indicate the author's opinion. Every effort is made to ensure that Greenhaven Press accurately reflects the original intent of the authors. Every effort has been made to trace the owners of copyrighted material.

Cover Image copyright Sandra G., 2009. Used under license from Shutterstock.com.

LIBRARY OF CONGRESS CATALOGING-IN-PUBLICATION DATA

White-collar crime / Kelly Wand, book editor.
    p. cm. -- (Opposing viewpoints)
  Includes bibliographical references and index.
  ISBN 978-0-7377-4548-1 (hardcover)
  ISBN 978-0-7377-4549-8 (pbk.)
  1. White collar crimes--United States. 2. Commercial crimes--United States.
3. Corporations--Corrupt practices--United States. I. Wand, Kelly.
  HV6769.W46 2009
  364.16'8--dc22

                         2009012401

Printed in the United States of America
1 2 3 4 5 6 7 13 12 11 10 09

Contents

Chapter 4: Is White-Collar Crime Institutionalized?

Why Consider Opposing Viewpoints?

> "The only way in which a human being can make some approach to knowing the whole of a subject is by hearing what can be said about it by persons of every variety of opinion and studying all modes in which it can be looked at by every character of mind. No wise man ever acquired his wisdom in any mode but this."
>
> John Stuart Mill

In our media-intensive culture it is not difficult to find differing opinions. Thousands of newspapers and magazines and dozens of radio and television talk shows resound with differing points of view. The difficulty lies in deciding which opinion to agree with and which "experts" seem the most credible. The more inundated we become with differing opinions and claims, the more essential it is to hone critical reading and thinking skills to evaluate these ideas. Opposing Viewpoints books address this problem directly by presenting stimulating debates that can be used to enhance and teach these skills. The varied opinions contained in each book examine many different aspects of a single issue. While examining these conveniently edited opposing views, readers can develop critical thinking skills such as the ability to compare and contrast authors' credibility, facts, argumentation styles, use of persuasive techniques, and other stylistic tools. In short, the Opposing Viewpoints Series is an ideal way to attain the higher-level thinking and reading skills so essential in a culture of diverse and contradictory opinions.

In addition to providing a tool for critical thinking, Opposing Viewpoints books challenge readers to question their own strongly held opinions and assumptions. Most people form their opinions on the basis of upbringing, peer pressure, and personal, cultural, or professional bias. By reading carefully balanced opposing views, readers must directly confront new ideas as well as the opinions of those with whom they disagree. This is not to simplistically argue that everyone who reads opposing views will—or should—change his or her opinion. Instead, the series enhances readers' understanding of their own views by encouraging confrontation with opposing ideas. Careful examination of others' views can lead to the readers' understanding of the logical inconsistencies in their own opinions, perspective on why they hold an opinion, and the consideration of the possibility that their opinion requires further evaluation.

Evaluating Other Opinions

To ensure that this type of examination occurs, Opposing Viewpoints books present all types of opinions. Prominent spokespeople on different sides of each issue as well as well-known professionals from many disciplines challenge the reader. An additional goal of the series is to provide a forum for other, less known, or even unpopular viewpoints. The opinion of an ordinary person who has had to make the decision to cut off life support from a terminally ill relative, for example, may be just as valuable and provide just as much insight as a medical ethicist's professional opinion. The editors have two additional purposes in including these less known views. One, the editors encourage readers to respect others' opinions—even when not enhanced by professional credibility. It is only by reading or listening to and objectively evaluating others' ideas that one can determine whether they are worthy of consideration. Two, the inclusion of such viewpoints encourages the important critical thinking skill of objectively evaluating an author's credentials and bias. This evaluation will illuminate an author's reasons for taking a particular stance on an issue and will aid in readers' evaluation of the author's ideas.

It is our hope that these books will give readers a deeper understanding of the issues debated and an appreciation of the complexity of even seemingly simple issues when good and honest people disagree. This awareness is particularly important in a democratic society such as ours in which people enter into public debate to determine the common good. Those with whom one disagrees should not be regarded as enemies but rather as people whose views deserve careful examination and may shed light on one's own.

Thomas Jefferson once said that "difference of opinion leads to inquiry, and inquiry to truth." Jefferson, a broadly educated man, argued that "if a nation expects to be ignorant and free . . . it expects what never was and never will be." As individuals and as a nation, it is imperative that we consider the opinions of others and examine them with skill and discernment. The Opposing Viewpoints Series is intended to help readers achieve this goal.

David L. Bender and Bruno Leone,
Founders

Introduction

"Ethics stays in the prefaces of the average business science book."

—*Peter Drucker,*
management consultant

Ever since 1960, when he founded his own securities firm in New York, Bernard Madoff was a widely respected member of the community. An eminent banker and the former chairman of the NASDAQ stock exchange, Madoff was also a generous donor to charitable causes, donating $2.5 million to Memorial Sloan Kettering Hospital and $1.7 million to the Leukemia and Lymphoma Society.

On December 10, 2008, Madoff confessed to his two sons Andrew and Mark that the asset management arm of the respected and powerful family securities firm was not only about to go bankrupt but for many years had been the instrument of a type of investment fraud known as a Ponzi scheme. Named after an early twentieth-century perpetrator, Charles Ponzi (who did not invent it), a Ponzi scheme is a fraudulent accounting scam in which investors are paid dividends using their own money or that of other investors rather than actual profits in order to get them to invest more. Ponzi schemes are particularly damaging forms of fraud since in addition to the duplicity factor, they require ever greater injections of cash to sustain the net losses, and therefore cannot be supported indefinitely. The greater the number of investors that become involved, the higher the risk of getting caught.

The revelation that Madoff's firm, which only weeks previously had been considered one of the most reputable businesses on Wall Street, came as a shock to many both in and beyond the financial industry, despite breaking at the tail end of a year that had already seen a $600 billion subprime mortgage crisis, the collapse of three of the world's largest banks in an avalanche of corporate scandals and mismanagement, Federal takeovers of two major securities firms, the possible dissolution of Detroit automakers, and the passage by Congress of a $700 billion bailout bill.

While the length of time that Madoff's scheme was in operation is still under debate, the Internal Revenue Service has estimated that his investors lost over $50 billion over the course of the last three decades. Upon receiving word of their staggering losses, two of Madoff's clients, William Foxton and René-Thierry Magon de la Villehuchet, committed suicide.

Madoff was arrested on December 11, 2008, by agents of the FBI and was released the same day after posting bail. Although he and his wife reportedly violated a court order freezing their assets by mailing up to $1 million in jewelry to Madoff's sons and brother, the judge refused to jail Madoff outside of assigning him to electronic monitoring and a 7 P.M. curfew at his residence.

While it seems doubtful that Madoff will ever work in the financial services industry again, federal prosecutors claim it is unlikely that much of the money he allegedly stole will ever be recovered. Currently Madoff faces having to pay up to $5 million in fines and spending up to twenty years in prison.

The Madoff case was just one in a long series of white-collar crime stories to come to light in 2008. Historically, more visually dramatic, violent crimes like bank robberies and high-speed police chases have dominated nightly news coverage. Yet in the past two years as the American economy has deteriorated to unanticipated levels, white-collar crime has gradually eclipsed other story types. The economy was considered the number one issue for American voters in the 2008 presidential election, even over the ongoing Iraq War, health insurance, and the threat of terrorism.

Although political corruption and predatory behavior by the wealthy have existed ever since the development of currency, the term "white-collar" itself originated in 1920, as a pejorative for affluent businessmen, referring to their white and starched collars as opposed to the "blue" work-shirts or protective clothing worn by manual laborers ("blue-collar").

But the phrase "white-collar crime" did not enter the public lexicon until 1949, when sociologist Edwin Sutherland first coined it to describe any "crime committed by a person of respectability and high social status in the course of his [or her] occupation." Sutherland's reasoning was that most financial crimes—such as bribery, fraud, forgery, and embezzlement—did not involve violence and therefore could only be committed by "white-collar" workers of relatively high income levels.

What constitutes a white-collar crime (or criminal) still remains a subject of debate. Environmentalists claim that the manufacture of inferior products, pollution, price fixing, and misleading adjectives like "diet" or "lite" in advertising serve as examples of white-collar crime. Others contend that the term refers only to the income class of the criminals themselves or that of the victims.

While precise definitions of white-collar crime may vary, few dispute the magnitude and devastating costs of white-collar crime not just to its victims but to society as a whole. According to criminologist Jeffrey Reiman, the cost of white-collar crime in 2000 (before the latest string of scandals and crises) was $404 billion, an estimate that only includes forms of conduct strictly defined as illegal. Many corporate activities that legally result in the deaths of American consumers or workers every year such as environmental pollution or the inclusion of permissible toxins in low-cost food products, prescription pharmaceuticals, or cigarettes are not accounted for in such figures.

In 2004, the Federal Bureau of Investigation estimated that identity theft, disaster fraud, and mortgage or credit card fraud cost taxpayers between $300 billion and $660 billion annually. The financial banking crisis of 2008 through 2009, the direct result of speculation, poorly managed bank debt, and insufficient regulation of the mortgage and securities industries that allowed alleged fraudsters like Madoff to flourish unmolested for such an extended period, triggered the passage of a $700 billion emergency bailout in October 2008, followed in February 2009 with a $787 billion stimulus act designed to begin rectifying the credit markets and national infrastructure damaged by the losses.

Some social critics, such as Noam Chomsky, argue that however pernicious one finds white-collar crime, it is an inevitable side effect of a capitalist economy founded on competitive principles. In this worldview, to have winners one must also have losers, whether they are the CEOs of ruthless companies or the buying public. According to Chomsky, corporations should be allowed to fail according to the same value system to which they adhered in times of prosperity.

Others believe that the system is not to blame but rather the lack of ethics exhibited by individuals themselves. While the vast majority of white-collar crimes victimize innocent people, many observers note that the American housing and financial crisis would never have attained such devastating scope without the avarice and compliance of American citizens who had become delinquent on mortgage payments that they had initially accepted even though they could not afford them.

Opposing Viewpoints: White-Collar Crime looks at this seemingly growing phenomenon under the following chapter titles: What Is White-Collar Crime? Who Commits White-Collar Crime? Is White-Collar Crime Appropriately Punished? and Is White-Collar Crime Institutionalized? The authors debate these topics and provide insights and information into this very current, very troubling issue.

OPPOSING
VIEWPOINTS®
SERIES

CHAPTER 1

What Is White-Collar Crime?

Chapter Preface

W hat exactly is a "white-collar" crime? Is a white-collar crime synonymous with corporate crime? Does the "whiteness" refer to the criminal, to the victims, or to the nature of the crime? Sixty years after the term was first coined by criminologist Edwin Sutherland to refer to "crime[s] committed by [persons] of respectability and high social status in the course of their occupations," students and scholars of the field, lawyers, and judges continue to disagree on the details.

Settling on a strict definition has become correspondingly more problematic as the ways in which people conduct commerce has become more diversified and complex. In Sutherland's day, e-mail and credit cards did not exist yet, let alone e-mail spam or electronic identity theft. Financial transactions took much longer to complete and relied principally on paperwork, teletype stock tickers, and personal meetings. Accounts were maintained in bound ledgers and filing cabinets. The same technological "paperless" advances like the Internet, cell phones, and online banking that have made life more convenient have ushered in with them a host of security issues, technical glitches, and accounting margins of error the likes of which members of Sutherland's generation could never have envisioned.

Yet although his original definition may strike us as overly narrow today, Sutherland's original claim that white-collar offenses warranted further study was a crucial milestone in the development of criminology.

The Federal Bureau of Investigation [FBI] characterizes white-collar crimes as "illegal acts [involving] deceit, concealment, or violation of trust and which are not dependent upon the application or threat of physical force." Some, like sociologist Neal Shover, suggest that the term applies strictly to the financial status of the perpetrators. Still others believe that only corporations, rather than individuals, can be accused of white-collar crime.

To further complicate matters, changing laws and public policies, coupled with a systematic effort by politicians and lobbyists for the last two decades to redefine what is legal and what is not, make consistent labeling even more challenging.

The viewpoints in the following chapter explore the various ways that white-collar crime is defined according to the opinions of those who study it, those who were victimized by it, and even those who claim that it does not exist at all.

> *"What is interesting and distinctive about [white-collar crime] is that, in a surprisingly large number of cases, there is a genuine doubt as to whether what the defendant was alleged to have done was in fact morally wrong."*

White-Collar Crime Is Morally Ambiguous

Stuart P. Green

Though few would argue that white-collar crime is wrong, Stuart P. Green, the author of the following viewpoint, argues that greater complexity and a number of other factors make it unique and often morally ambiguous. Green notes that even in high-profile cases, white-collar offenders tend to be committing acts that many in the business industry consider merely "aggressive" and for all intents legal. Other issues include the tricky nature of defining the victims and sums involved, the means of establishing criminal intent, and the often arbitrary ways white-collar cases are both prosecuted and covered in the media.

Stuart P. Green is a scholar of criminal law. His books include Lying, Cheating, and Stealing: A Moral Theory of White

Stuart P. Green, "Moral Ambiguity in White Collar Criminal Law," *Notre Dame Journal of Law, Ethics, and Public Policy*, vol. 18, Summer 2004, pp. 501–519. Reproduced by permission.

Collar Crime *and, as coeditor,* Defining Crimes: Essays on the Special Part of the Criminal Law.

As you read, consider the following questions:

1. In what way does the author claim that it is legally challenging to distinguish between criminality and "merely aggressive" behavior?

2. What does Green cite as an example of the difficulty in ascribing the "harm" caused by white-collar crime compared with street crime?

3. What is "mens rea" and what, according to the author, makes it hard to establish with regard to white-collar crime?

Criminal sanctions, the most serious kind of sanctions we have in a civil society, have traditionally been reserved for conduct that not only causes or risks serious harms but is also unambiguously wrongful.

In some unusual cases involving necessity or other justification defenses, a defendant might argue that killing another human being or causing some other serious harm was the right thing to do. But in the typical case of core criminal offenses such as murder, rape, and robbery, there is an underlying assumption that what the defendant did—if in fact she did do it—was, from a moral perspective, a very bad thing. There is, however, an important collection of criminal offenses that reflects a different pattern. The offenses I have in mind—bribery, extortion, fraud, tax evasion, perjury, obstruction of justice, false statements, insider trading, and various regulatory and intellectual property crimes—tend to be committed without violence; the harms they cause are often diffuse; and the victims they affect are frequently hard to identify. For lack of a better term, and while recognizing its contested nature, I will refer to this rather loosely defined "family" of offenses as "white collar" crimes.

What is interesting and distinctive about this group of crimes is that, in a surprisingly large number of cases, there is a genuine doubt as to whether what the defendant was alleged to have done was in fact morally wrong. In such cases, the issue is not, as it is with necessity, whether the defendant was confronted with some extraordinary choice between either obeying the law, and allowing significant harm to occur; or violating the law, and preventing such harm.

Rather, the question is whether the conduct engaged in was more or less acceptable behavior, at least in the realm in which it was performed, and therefore, should not have been subject to criminal sanctions in the first place. Such ambiguity reflects more than just the effectiveness of white collar defense counsel in promoting their clients' causes, although the influence of defense counsel in such cases is surely significant. In fact, it reflects a more widespread sense—expressed by judges, jurors, scholars, journalists, and the average citizen—that there is a kind of moral complexity and uncertainty in such offenses that is rarely seen in the case of more traditional crimes. This ambiguity has frequently been remarked upon, but there have been few systematic attempts to explain exactly how or why it occurs. . . .

Examples of Moral Ambiguity

The kind of moral ambiguity I have in mind is illustrated by the following cases:

In November 2003, Clarence Norman, chairman of the Brooklyn Democratic Party, and Jeffrey Feldman, the Party's Executive Director, were indicted on what amounted to charges of extortion.

There is little dispute that Norman and Feldman had met with candidates running for civil court judge and told them that they would not receive the party's wholehearted support unless they used certain selected vendors and consultants.

But there is serious disagreement about the criminality of such conduct. According to Brooklyn District Attorney Charles Hynes, such conduct constitutes the very "definition [of] extortion."

According to lawyers for Norman and Feldman, as well as various prominent political figures in Brooklyn, however, there was nothing illegal about what the defendants did. As Norman's lawyer, Roger Bennet Adler put it,

> If you take [the allegations] at face value ... imposing certain conditions on candidates running on a joint slate, there was nothing unreasonable about those conditions. Suggesting that if you don't basically agree to these expenditures we're not going to be as effective for you on primary day, I think, is a statement of the obvious. It's not extortion.

In June 2002, the Arthur Andersen accounting firm was convicted of obstructing the Securities and Exchange Commission's [SEC's] investigation into the collapse of Enron.

Among the pieces of evidence that jurors found most incriminating was an email from in-house Andersen lawyer, Nancy Temple, instructing Andersen partner, David Duncan, to remove language from an internal Andersen memo suggesting that Andersen had concluded that an earlier Enron final disclosure had been misleading.

The email also advised Duncan to remove any reference to consultations with Andersen's in-house legal team, saying it could be considered a waiver of attorney-client privilege. According to one of the jurors, "[w]e wanted to find Andersen not guilty and find that they stood up to Enron. But it's clear [that Temple] knew investigators were coming and was telling [Andersen] to alter the evidence."

Yet not everyone agreed with the jury's interpretation. Several days after the Andersen trial ended, Stephen Gillers, a leading professor of legal ethics, opined on the op-ed page of the *New York Times* that the advice Temple had given to the accounting firm was not a crime at all, but rather "the kind of advice lawyers give clients all the time."

More Examples

In 2001, computer programmer Dmitry Sklyarov and his firm, ElcomSoft, became the first defendants charged with violating criminal provisions of the 1998 Digital Millennium Copyright Act (DMCA), which are intended to prevent the circumvention of technological protections on copyrighted material.

Sklyarov had cracked the technological protection measure used by Adobe Systems to control access to copyrighted content distributed in its eBook format. The prosecution of Sklyarov was widely criticized by civil liberties groups such as the Electronic Frontier Foundation, who maintained that the DMCA violates First Amendment rights and hinders technological innovation. Sklyarov was successful in having the charges against him dropped in return for his agreeing to testify against ElcomSoft. The case against ElcomSoft proceeded to trial, where the firm was acquitted. The jury believed that ElcomSoft's product did violate the law, but apparently nullified the verdict based on its belief that ElcomSoft and Sklyarov had done nothing morally wrong.

Between 1995 and 1999, executives at two of the largest seed companies in the world, Monsanto and Pioneer Hi-Bred International, met repeatedly and agreed to charge higher prices for genetically modified seeds.

The talks between the two companies involved licenses that allowed Pioneer to sell altered seeds developed by Monsanto. To the extent that the companies discussed prices, swapped profit projections, and talked about cooperating to keep the prices of genetically modified seeds high, one might think that they [had] violated the criminal price-fixing provisions of the Sherman Antitrust Act. Yet, according to a spokesman for Monsanto, "[i]n the context of a potentially new license for technology, it is absolutely within the law to discuss the price and the means of compensation to the licensing party."

In October 2003, Mikhail Khodorkovsky, the chief executive and principal owner of Russia's largest oil company, Yukos, was arrested and charged with tax evasion and related offenses.

A few days later, Leon Aron, director of Russian studies at the American Enterprise Institute, published an op-ed piece in the *New York Times* arguing that, while Khodorkovsky may have "broke[n] some laws ... in the chaotic Russian economy of the [1990s], when the state was privatizing its assets on a grand scale, no large business was 'clean'—and the larger the company, the greater the chance it committed violations."

According to Aron, given the tax scheme then in force in Russia, "[t]ax evasion was the only strategy that allowed an entrepreneur to pay salaries and invest in his business."

In what sense do the foregoing cases involve moral ambiguity? Are there different forms of ambiguity that they reflect? What causes such ambiguity? What are its effects? Does the ambiguity reflect the way in which we regard the people who engage in such acts, or the way we perceive the acts themselves? Does such ambiguity pose a problem for the criminal law? Can the problem be fixed? Each of the five cases identified above is complex, and generalizations are bound to be difficult. They involve a wide range of quite different statutes, perpetrators, victims, harms, and mitigating and aggravating circumstances. . . .

Difficult to Distinguish

Everyone, or almost everyone, would agree that certain core cases of bribery, fraud, tax evasion, obstruction of justice, perjury, and extortion involve conduct that is morally wrongful; and that if such conduct is proven, it should be treated as criminal. For example, if the Brooklyn Democratic Party bosses referred to above had threatened to bankrupt anyone who failed to use their favored vendors, there would be little doubt that they would have committed a serious crime and would deserve to be punished. The problem is that much white collar crime is not nearly so straightforward. Many instances of alleged extortion, fraud, and similar offenses are difficult to distinguish from conduct that involves "merely aggressive" business, litigation, or political behavior. In such cases, it may seem that: what is alleged to be extortion was nothing more than "hardball negotiating"; what prosecutors call obstruction of justice was actually just "zealous advocacy"; what an indictment refers to as perjury was really just "wiliness" on the witness stand; what is alleged to be fraud was merely "creative accounting"; what a criminal complaint calls tax evasion was in fact legal tax "avoidance"; what prosecutors consider a bribe was merely a "campaign contribution," and so on. Conventional street crime rarely exhibits such ambiguities. . . .

In contrast to offenses such as fraud, perjury, and extortion, there is a group of offenses involving conduct that—even in the most hard-core cases—is not universally viewed as morally wrongful. For example, there is significant debate over whether it should be a crime to engage in: (1) insider trading; (2) various so-called *malum prohibitum* [prohibited evil] regulatory offenses, such as taking sleeping pills without a prescription, carrying a gun without a permit, and selling liquor without a license; and (3) various intellectual property offenses, such as criminal copyright and trademark infringement, theft of trade secrets, and the manufacture and sale of devices that can be used to circumvent technological protection measures (the last of which being the offense with which Dmitry Sklyarov was charged).

"Overcriminalization"

All of these are areas in which "overcriminalization" has been said to occur. The problem is particularly striking in the intellectual property area. Recent studies have shown that more

27

than 70% of people polled do not believe it is wrong to make unauthorized photocopies of a book or magazine, more than half do not regard the unauthorized downloading of music as immoral, 49% do not think it is wrong to make unauthorized copies of CDs and tapes, 35% do not believe it is wrong to make unauthorized copies of videocassettes, and 25% do not believe it is wrong to make unauthorized copies of computer software.

In what sense, then, are offenses like these morally ambiguous? By labeling and punishing certain conduct as "criminal," our legal system sends a message that such conduct is worthy of censure.

When such labeling is consistent with what society as a whole regards as morally wrongful, law and norms are mutually reinforcing. But when there is a gap between what the law regards as morally wrongful and what a significant segment of society views as such—that is, where norms become "sticky,"—moral conflict and ambiguity are likely to be the result.

Defining Harms and Identifying Victims

Most of the white collar offenses we are concerned with here can be distinguished from traditional street crimes in that they tend to involve more complex forms of underlying activity, harder-to-discern harms, and harder-to-identify victims. Like the alleged price fixing between Monsanto and Pioneer, white collar offenses often occur over an extended period of time and involve elaborate activities such as those associated with manufacturing and industrial processes, marketing, corporate finance, the stock market, so-called document retention procedures, government contracts, financial auditing, trial and litigation procedures, and political fundraising. Such activity frequently occurs within large and complex organizations, involving numerous individuals occupying a wide range of different positions, and many series of complicated transactions. Understanding how such processes work can require a fairly sophisticated understanding of disciplines such as finance, economics, engineering, medicine, political science, organizational theory, management, accounting, environmental science, and information technology. It is often hard enough for the lay public to understand how these processes are supposed to work when they are conducted in a legal manner; it is all the more difficult to understand how they function when they involve criminal activity. Because the context in which white collar crime occurs is often so complex, it can be difficult to understand exactly how a defendant has violated a given criminal provision.

White collar offenses also tend to involve harms that are more difficult to identify than in the case of conventional street crimes. For example, there is not likely to be much controversy about the proposition that the principal harm caused by homicide is the death of a human being. In the case of crimes such as tax evasion, bribery, and insider trading, by contrast, the identification of harm and victim presents real difficulties. Some direct harms seem relatively straightforward; presumably, tax evasion leads to reduced revenues for the public treasury, bribery to biased governmental decision making, and insider trading to loss of money for some investors. But there are also significant indirect, diffuse, and aggregative harms caused by such conduct, which are much harder to quantify—e.g., loss of investor and consumer confidence, distrust of government, and bad decisions made by public officials.

Given the diffuseness of harms associated with white collar offenses, it is not surprising that identification of affected victims is also harder than in the case of conventional offenses.

For example, while we have no problem in saying that the principal victim of homicide is the decedent, it is difficult to say exactly which citizens are victimized by environmental violations and government corruption; which taxpayers are victimized by false claims and tax evasion; which employees are victimized by labor law violations and the devastation of their retirement accounts; and which consumers are victimized by price fixing, violations of the food and drug and product safety laws, and fraudulent marketing practices. Many white collar crimes involve small harms to a large number of victims, and are significant only in the aggregate.

And, of course, some victims of white collar crime are never even aware that they have been victimized.

All this complexity of underlying conduct and difficulty in identifying harms and victims contributes inevitably to moral ambiguity. If people find it hard to recognize what kinds of harms a particular offense causes, or who suffers them, they are likely to be less certain that such conduct is wrong and should be subject to sanctions.

Diffusion of Responsibility

Not only does white collar crime present difficulties in assessing the means by which it is committed, the harms it causes, and the victims it affects, but there are also problems in determining exactly who (or what, in the case of an entity) should be held responsible. Many of the offenses referred to above are most likely to occur within the context of complex institutions, such as large corporations, partnerships, and government agencies. In such organizations, responsibility for decision making and implementation is shared among boards of directors, shareholders, top and mid-level managers, and ground-level employees.

As a result, the blame we attribute to an individual actor within the organization in which he works may be less than the blame we attribute to an individual actor committing an equally serious street crime on his own. Consider again the case of Arthur Andersen.

Prior to its demise, Andersen was one of the "big five" international accounting firms, with more than 25,000 employ-

Problem of Physical Evidence

In the context of white collar crime, the cost imposed by the liberal features of the criminal law is especially high. To see why, imagine what the position of a federal prosecutor charged with combating white collar crime would be if he or she were burdened with the substantive and procedural safeguards of the traditional criminal law. First, consider the effect that the presumption of innocence and the requirement of proof beyond reasonable doubt would have on his or her efforts.... Policing all of the business concerns in the United States not only for honest dealing, but for compliance with the myriad regulations that carry criminal penalties is a truly monumental task. No matter how large the [Department of Justice] budget for white collar crime may be, it would still be insufficient to address anything beyond the tip of the iceberg of potential offenses. Furthermore, white collar crime typically consists of deceptive behavior. There is usually no ... smoking gun to introduce into evidence. White collar criminal activity is intentionally designed to be indistinguishable from non-criminal activity. As a result, considerable investigation may be required merely to establish that a crime has been committed....

The greatest challenge our prosecutor would face, however, is likely to be presented by the attorney-client privilege and the right against self-incrimination. As noted above, because white collar crime consists primarily of crimes of deception, the type of physical evidence associated with traditional criminal activity is rarely available. The evidence upon which conviction for a white collar offense must rest will be almost entirely documentary in nature, and will consist predominantly of the business records of the firm for which the defendant works. But to the extent that these records are in the personal possession of the defendant, contain communications between the defendant or other members of the firm and corporate counsel, or are the work product of corporate counsel, the right against self-incrimination and the attorney-client privilege render them unavailable to the prosecution.... The evidence necessary for a conviction for a white collar criminal offense will be in the hands of those who cannot be compelled to produce it.

John Hasnas, American University Law Review, *2005.*

ees in the United States alone, and thousands more employees working at affiliated offices around the world. According to the indictment charging Andersen with obstruction of justice, documents were allegedly destroyed not only in Houston, but also in London, Chicago, and Portland, Oregon. The order to destroy the documents came from within a complex corporate hierarchy and was carried out by hundreds of employees. A low-level secretary or clerk who shredded documents knowing that they would be subject to an SEC subpoena would surely deserve blame for his conduct. But our judgment of such a person would likely be tempered—made more ambivalent, I would say—by the fact that the person acted within the context of a large organization and shared responsibility with numerous other actors. . . .

Distinctive Role for Mens Rea

Mens rea, or "guilty mind," reflects one of the defining characteristics of criminal law. Many serious harms caused without mental intent provide grounds for civil liability, but they do not traditionally give rise to criminal prosecution. The criminal law has traditionally required not only that the defendant cause a serious harm (the *actus reus* [guilty act]) but also that she do so with a particular state of mind—criminal intent, purpose, knowledge, belief, recklessness, or the like. People who cause harm without such mental element ordinarily cannot be said to be "at fault" or "deserving" in the way that the just imposition of punishment is thought to require.

In the case of many white collar crimes, however, the requirement of mens rea is stood on its head. Some of the offenses—particularly in the area of regulatory crime—require either no mens rea at all (i.e., they are strict liability offenses), or they require a low level form of mens rea, such as negligence. And because of such dilution of the mens rea requirement, it is difficult to say that the perpetrators of such offenses are morally culpable, or at least culpable to the extent that would justify the imposition of criminal penalties.

Other white collar offenses present a converse problem: proof of mens rea is so crucial to their definition that conduct performed without it not only fails to expose the actor to criminal (as opposed to civil) liability, but is not regarded as wrongful at all. Consider, for example, the case of bribery. Imagine that X, a constituent of Congressman Y, gives Y a certain amount of money (which, we can further assume, falls within the amounts permissible under campaign finance laws). Assuming that X acts with the expectation of receiving nothing in return, he has committed no offense; he has merely made a legal campaign contribution. X's act of giving money to Y would constitute a bribe if and only if X "corruptly . . . inten[ded] to influence" an official act.

The problem, however, is that it is notoriously difficult to determine whether an actor acted with corrupt intent. In light of such difficulties, it is not surprising that such conduct is often viewed as morally ambiguous.

Value of Surrounding Legitimate Conduct

Most of the offenses I have been considering are committed in the course of conduct that is otherwise legal, and even socially productive. Government officials who accept bribes are frequently also involved in legitimate governmental functions; investors who trade on the basis of inside information tend to be engaged in legal investment as well; and people who commit regulatory and intellectual property crimes are often engaged in the business of producing valuable products and services. Mikhail Khodorkovsky, for example, is not only one of the richest men in Russia and head of its largest oil company, but also an important symbol of Russia's transition to a capitalist economy, and a hero to many. In some cases, such people even use their wealth for worthwhile philanthropic purposes.

The same cannot generally be said in the case of drug dealers, burglars, and serial killers (although there are surely exceptions). To the extent that a perpetrator's criminal conduct is likely to be judged in light of, and balanced against, her socially beneficial conduct, ambiguity is once again likely to be the result.

Legislative Attitudes

Our judgment of whether and to what extent various forms of conduct are morally wrong is undoubtedly influenced by how such conduct is treated by the law.

Indeed, there are, in addition to the criminalization of ostensibly morally neutral conduct referred to above, at least four other ways in which legislatures have contributed to the phenomenon of moral ambiguity in white collar crime. First, many of the crimes we have been considering are dealt with in specialized, regulatory portions of state and federal law rather than in the criminal law proper. For example, securities fraud is dealt with in the part of the U.S. Code dealing with securities law, tax evasion in sections dealing with tax law, criminal price-fixing in the antitrust provisions, and environmental crimes in the titles dealing with environmental law. Because such offenses are codified separately from "real crimes," they are perhaps less likely to be thought of as real crimes.

Second, most of the offenses we have been talking about are enforceable by means of both criminal prosecution and private or governmental civil actions. Indeed, it has been suggested that, in the case of certain forms of white collar wrongdoing, criminal law may even be the less preferred approach.

Such "hybrid" criminal/civil character is particularly evident under regulatory-type statutes such as the Securities Exchange Act of 1934, the Sherman Act, Clean Water Act, Bankruptcy Code, Tax Code, Truth in Lending Act, False Claims Act, and Federal Food, Drug and Cosmetic Act.

Under such statutes, precisely the same conduct can give rise to either criminal or civil penalties, with the discretion to pursue one or the other wholly in the hands of prosecuting officials. The result is that the line between white collar crime and non-criminal cases becomes blurred, even arbitrary. Third, under federal law, some criminal statutes contain a "morally neutral" element that must be satisfied in order for federal jurisdiction to be established. For example, under the mail fraud statute, the government must prove that the defendant "place[d] in any post office or authorized depository for mail matter, any matter or thing whatever to be sent or delivered by the Postal Service."

Because the government must present evidence that the defendant engaged in the morally neutral act of mailing a letter, some observers may be left with the impression that the larger mail fraud prosecution itself involves a morally ambiguous act.

Fourth, a reasonable case could be made that legislatures have tended to authorize (and judges to impose) less severe penalties for white collar offenses than for equally or less serious street crimes.

Admittedly, comparing white collar and non–white collar crimes in terms of seriousness is bound to be difficult. Nevertheless, one cannot help but be struck by U.S. Sentencing Commission statistics indicating that, during 2001, the average sentence for white collar crime was just over 20 months, while the average sentence for drug and violent crimes was 71.7 and 89.5 months, respectively.

And there is plenty of anecdotal evidence to the same effect; to cite just one example, in the late 1990s, officials of Archer Daniels Midland were caught red-handed on videotape rigging prices of agricultural products with competitors. The trial judge sentenced the two ringleaders to a mere two years in prison each. An outraged appeals court increased the sentence to the statutory maximum of three years. Even so, as [investigative reporter] Kurt Eichenwald has put it, the result was that "executives who effectively cheated every grocery store in the country received shorter sentences than if they had robbed just one."

Prosecutorial and Judicial Attitudes

Moral ambiguity in white collar crime is fostered not only by legislative bodies, but also by judges and prosecutors. In the case of judges, one can observe an interesting inversion in attitudes, apparently based on political ideology and class consciousness: "conservative" judges tend to be more aggressive than their "liberal counterparts in their attitudes toward the investigation, prosecution, and punishment of street crime; in the case of white collar offenses, just the opposite is true."

To the extent that people take their cues from judicial decisions, the result is likely to be a certain amount of confusion. There is also evidence to suggest that prosecutors are likely to be more lenient with respect to white collar crime than in the case of street crime. A striking example is provided by a recent study of the federal Occupational Safety and Health Administration (OSHA).

During the period from 1982 to 2002, the agency investigated 1,242 cases in which it concluded that workers had died because of "willful" safety violations on part of their employers. All of these cases would seem to have involved a violation of criminal law. Yet in *ninety-three percent* of the cases, OSHA declined to prosecute, apparently owing to a "culture of reluctance [that] rules [the agency] regardless of which party controls Congress or the White House."

Just as the public takes its cues from the legislative treatment of white collar crime, so too is it influenced by how such crime is treated by prosecutors and in the courts. If white collar crime is *treated* as less serious than street crime, it is not surprising that people tend to think of it as less serious than such crime. . . .

Other Influences on Public Attitudes

Public attitudes towards white collar crime are affected not only by how such offenses are treated by government officials, but also by the criminal defense bar, the media, the public relations industry, and the academy. Defendants in white collar criminal cases are much more likely than those in street crime cases to have the money to hire lawyers, investigators, paralegals, jury consultants, and others to assist in their cause. Highly paid white collar criminal defense lawyers are more successful at almost every stage in the criminal justice process than their public defender counterparts. They do a better job of persuading to help repair reputations damaged by allegations of criminal conduct.

All of those retained are expert at exploiting the moral ambiguity of white collar crime, whether at trial or in the larger court of public opinion. The seriousness of white collar crime also tends to be minimized by the media. Both newspapers and broadcast media tend to give more attention to conventional, interpersonal, sensational, and violent forms of criminality than to their more subtle white collar counterparts.

The more limited media coverage of such crimes seems to be attributable to the complexity and supposed "dullness" of the conduct involved, the more indirect nature of the harm experienced by individual victims, and the fact that such criminality tends to produce fewer striking visual images on which television news in particular thrives.

In addition, it may be that media organizations are more likely to be intimidated in their coverage of white collar crime by the possibility that corporate sponsors might withdraw advertising and that deep-pocketed targets of white collar investigations might institute defamation suits.

Finally, it is worth noting that the academic treatment of white collar crime may also contribute to its morally ambiguous character. Criminologists going back to Edwin Sutherland have complained that their colleagues neglect white collar criminality in favor of street crime. A similar phenomenon can be observed in the law schools. White collar offenses are almost never dealt with in introductory courses in criminal law, and are only rarely mentioned in the general literature on criminal law theory. There are of course courses in "white collar" and "federal" crime that deal with offenses such as mail fraud, perjury, and obstruction. But to the extent that law school curricula deal at all with the subject of regulatory crime, it is only in passing, in more general courses on environmental, tax, securities, antitrust, intellectual property, labor, and administrative law. The result is that such offenses (if not white collar crime more generally) tend to be viewed more as "violations" than as genuine "crimes."

The Ambiguity of Ambiguity

Assuming that white collar crime really does reflect the kind of moral ambiguity I have been describing, two questions naturally arise: First, is moral ambiguity a bad thing? Second, assuming that it is, what can be done about it? Although ambiguity might in some cases mean flexibility, it is surely not a phenomenon that, as a general matter, should be encouraged. Our system is committed to the notion that only the most clearly harmful and wrongful kinds of conduct should be treated with criminal sanctions. Such sanctions need to be applied sparingly, consistently, and with a clearly articulated rationale. If our attitudes towards white collar crime are too ambiguous, the moral authority of the criminal law will itself be viewed as ambiguous. How, then, can such ambiguity be reduced? A number of reforms could certainly be considered: We could insist that legislatures avoid criminalizing conduct the moral wrongfulness of which is the subject of serious controversy. We could require legislatures to distinguish clearly between inchoate and completed conduct, and insist on a showing of mens rea for all crimes. We could endeavor to define the harms caused by, and the victims of, white collar crime more clearly than is done under current law. We could seek ways to integrate white collar crime more fully into our criminal codes, create sentencing parity between comparable white collar and conventional offenses, and require greater evenhandedness in terms of prosecutorial and judicial attitudes. We could demand that conduct resulting in criminal liability be distinguished more clearly from conduct resulting in civil liability. And we could formulate rules to determine more clearly how criminal responsibility should be attributed to individuals working within large organizations.

But even if all of these reforms could be effected, there would, I believe, remain an unavoidable element of moral ambiguity deeply embedded in the fabric of white collar criminal law.

Much of white collar crime involves conduct that is hard to define, hard to identify, and hard to prove; yet it is also some of the most harmful conduct our society faces. The answer is not a retreat from the criminalization of such conduct, but rather a recognition of its distinctive character, and a resolve to seek out certainty where ambiguity now prevails.

> "Many corporate offences are just plain
> evil incarnate and cause horrible hurt
> and damage."

White-Collar Crime Is Morally Wrong

Harry Glasbeek

While many within the business industry discount the significance and frequency of white-collar crimes, Harry Glasbeek, the author of the following viewpoint, argues that such crimes are both common and in some cases highly destructive. Glasbeek notes that the slippery nature of corporation status entitles companies to legal protections that exempt individuals working within them from blame for any wrongdoing. While many white-collar crimes are difficult for average citizens to analyze and are regarded by those within the corporate culture as a "natural side effect" of competitive market forces, Glasbeek charges that this unapologetically cutthroat environment tends to breed acts of callous immorality, including continuing to sell dangerous products because paying damages is cheaper than recalling them.

Harry Glasbeek is professor emeritus of Osgoode Hall Law School at York University in Toronto and the author of Wealth by Stealth.

As you read, consider the following questions:

1. According to the author, how does a corporation function as a businessperson's "invisible friend"?

2. What are two examples cited by Glasbeek of corporations knowingly lying about a faulty product even after doing so led to human deaths?

3. In the author's view, what are two advantages of "the corporate form" compared to the rights enjoyed by workers?

Publicly traded corporations: they are everywhere. They talk to us. They support political causes, parties and politicians. They sponsor opera, ballet, theatre, tennis, football, hospitals and universities. They are renaissance operations. They employ us. They sack us. They maim and kill us. They ravage and rape our physical and spiritual environments. They are the embodiment of capitalism. They protect capitalists from being held to account.

The legal architecture of the Anglo-American corporation ensures crimes can be and will be committed on behalf of the rich. This corporate veil is woven to hide the rich from our gaze—behind this veil they do us harm and render our numerical majority relatively impotent.

Once wealth-owners contribute capital to a firm, they incorporate as a legal corporation, and they are then given a certificate (ie, stocks) that gives them the right to participate in the appointment of the directors and managers who are to deploy the now "collectivized" capital so as to maximize profits. The registered corporation is deemed to be a separate legal person, acting in its own right. The contributors who hold the certificates are entitled to share in the profits according to the number they own and may vote at some decision-making meetings about corporate policy. They are also entitled to share in any property left over after the corporation ends business and has paid all its debts. They have traded their property-owning status over their capital for the privilege of limited liability. This means simply that, should the corporation be unable to pay for any damages done or debts incurred while chasing profits, these shareholders cannot be personally called upon to make further contributions. Their only financial risk is the potential loss of their initial investment—a very limited risk when dealing with large publicly traded corporations. If things don't look good, the owner of the certificate can sell it at any time.

Legal Fictions

This is how it works. According to legal fiction, once a venture is registered as a corporation, a new property-owning and investing "person" is created. This is the investors' "invisible friend." The harms inflicted by the venture can then be attributed to this new "person" (i.e., the corporation), not to individual investors. This corporate "person" is separate from the shareholders who stand to benefit from its profit-chasing activities. Shareholders are protected from fiscal losses in a way that no other market actor could hope for. They are also rendered legally immune from any wrongful, illegal and criminal acts the corporation might commit in their search for profits. They are like children who can claim, with perfect legality, "It wasn't me!"

Children often invent invisible friends to take the blame when they misbehave. But kids grow up and, as they mature, they are taught to take responsibility for their own conduct. Not so for the titans of capitalism who continue to blame their "invisible friend" (i.e., the corporation) who commits crimes on their behalf. This is how the corporation is designed in law to create a class of legally irresponsible profit-maximizers. They have no reason to care about the way in which profits are garnered by their creature, the corporation. Indeed, there is an incentive to have the corporation act wrongfully, illegally and criminally if that pays!

But despite the pretence that a corporation is a real person, unlike you and I it has no physical, corporate body that can think and act. Live human beings have to do that for it. But when they think and act on behalf of their corporate bodies, they can claim that they are not acting as people in their own right, but as the corporation. It's a short step to the claim that they are not *personally* responsible for any thinking and acting that might do harm and/or breach a law.

True, sometimes directors/managers are held responsible if it can be determined that their thoughts and acts are their own, rather than those of the corporation. But the starting position is that senior managers have a measure of immunity, although not quite the privilege of total legal irresponsibility enjoyed by the shareholders. The senior managers' prestige and rewards tend to rely on improving the value of the shareholders' interests. This will encourage wrongful corporate behaviour if it is likely to pay off in increased shareholder satisfaction.

Innocent Even If Guilty

Then there is the legal flipside. Because the corporation needs others to think and act, it cannot be guilty of a criminal offence. There is no wrongdoer whose intention to commit an illegal act can be proved. No one seems responsible—not the senior management, not the shareholder, not the corporation. To get around this, the law is forced to use another pretence: it holds the corporation "criminally responsible" when its acting mind and will exhibit wrongful intention. In a large corporation, this is immensely difficult to prove. It helps immunize corporations from criminal prosecutions and increases incentive for wrongdoing—if it pays.

Corporations commit an enormous number of offences. One conservative study notes that 60 per cent of Fortune 500 companies are convicted of an offence annually. Many of them are common misdemeanours—not getting a permit or a

Defining Business Ethics

Understanding the landscape of business ethics can be problematic. The field is vast, often encompassing such concerns as corporate governance, reputation management, accurate accounting and audits, fair labor practices and environmental stewardship to name but a few. In fact, the field addresses the entire scope of responsibilities—or obligations—that a company has to each of its stakeholders: those who have a vested interest—or stake—in the decisions and actions of a company, like clients, employees, shareholders, suppliers and the community. Depending upon the company in question, one may even be able to identify additional stakeholders.

The field of business ethics is further complicated by the fact that many terms exist to refer to corporate offices and programs intended to communicate, monitor, and enforce a company's values and standards. In theory, one can make some rough distinctions among the various domains related to business ethics, e.g., corporate responsibility, social responsibility, corporate compliance, etc. In practice, however, such distinctions blur.

International Business Ethics Institute, 2005.

licence, failure to record or publish information, not getting appropriate insurance coverage. These do not lead to the clamour for revenge inspired by common street crime. But many corporate offences are just plain evil incarnate and cause horrible hurt and damage.

The examples are endless. British American Tobacco and Philip Morris knowingly lied about a product—tobacco—that led to addiction and killed their customers. The World Health Organization estimates four million people die yearly from tobacco-related illness. No one has been tried for this conscious infliction of terrible hurt. Johns-Manville and the Cape Company knowingly exposed millions of people to poisonous asbestos. Some 18 per cent of serious exposures are estimated to result in life-threatening disease. They lied to governments and workers as they chased profits at the expense of life. No one has been charged with a criminal offense. The manufacturer A.H. Robins knew that its intrauterine contraceptive device would let loose organ-affecting bacteria when inserted in women. Many miscarriages and some deaths later, they went into bankruptcy—but no one was ever prosecuted for this wilful infliction of harm. Nestlé hustled women in poor countries to use their powdered milk, instead of breastmilk. When the powder was mixed with impure water, large numbers of babies got sick. Some died. If Nestlé did not comprehend this at first, protesters brought it to their attention. Yet they persisted in their quest for profits at the cost of babies' lives for many years. No charges.

Ford made a Pinto car that exploded on touch. It had known this could happen, but preferred not to cut into its profits by recalling the car—paying damages to the burnt victims was cheaper. No one was ever convicted for these deaths by immolation.

Royal Dutch Shell, Unocal, Talisman and Occidental Petroleum have been implicated in the murderous practices of various repressive regimes in Aceh, Nigeria, Burma, Sudan and Colombia. The poisoning of the Love Canal community in upper New York State was brought to us by a subsidiary of Occidental Petroleum; the mass gassing of Bhopal, by a subsidiary of Union Carbide.

The rate of recidivism (reoffending) is truly spectacular. Take ExxonMobil, who despoiled the pristine Alaska coast with sticky black oil and then saw their recklessly engineered gas plant in Australia explode, killing workers and leaving a whole state without gas for three weeks; then in Alabama these oil barons deliberately scammed the Government out of $3.5 billion and went on to steal fresh water from New York's Hudson River and replace it with polluting bilge. Firestone made the tires for Ford's SUVs. The deaths caused when the SUVs flipped are blamed on tire defects by Ford and SUV engineering by Firestone. In the 1970s Firestone produced steel-belted radials that it knew had a tendency to separate—with some 24 million of them on the road at least 41 people were killed and many more were injured when the tires blew out. I could go on and on.

The Corporate Norm

Corporate evildoing is not exceptional behaviour: rather, it is the norm. The corporation has been legally designed as a criminogenic creature—in other words, prone to compulsive criminal behaviour. The law devised a scheme of business regulatory rules that penalizes offenders without criminalizing them. The idea is that corporate offences are not real crimes, but "overly aggressive behaviour"—a natural side effect of being a competitive market actor that generates the wealth we all share. Such offences, so the thinking goes, are of a lesser order and should not stigmatize violators.

It is now becoming more common to hold senior managers personally responsible for their corporations' wrongdoing. This is to be welcomed because it finally recognizes that real flesh-and-blood human beings are responsible for corporate conduct. But the key issue is: why do these bloodless corporations commit so many wrongs? The hub of the matter—the structured criminogenic nature of the corporation—is avoided. Meanwhile governments go through elaborate gymnastics to prove their even-handed application of our laws and values.

In 1996 the English Law Commission recommended a new law against corporate killing. Despite the law being backed repeatedly by the Labour Government, it has not as yet acted on the suggestion. In Australia, the Federal Government passed legislation making a corporation, as such, criminally responsible if its culture led to the commission of a crime. Similar legislation is under consideration in Canada and by two Australian state governments. A few steps in the right direction— these events are now seen as more than just a regulatory peccadillo. But the protected rapaciousness of the wealth-owning class still hides behind the corporate veil.

The corporate form allows wealth-owners to influence governments more effectively than they could as simple individuals. It leaves them better placed to lord it over small entrepreneurs, consumers and workers. Workers' right to combine in unions faces serious restrictions on the use of their collectivized power. No such constraints are imposed on shareholders who are given limited fiscal liability and total legal immunity. Corporate managers are expected to do everything in their power to maximize the wealth of the protected shareholders.

Corporate criminality is but a manifestation of the brutality of capitalist relations of production. We need to see shareholders for what they are, beneficiaries of the killing, maiming and ravaging of our cultural, physical and political environments. This is a first step in demystifying the way in which capitalism maintains its legitimacy. There is an entirely plausible argument to be made that criminal law should hold major shareholders responsible for the many evils done by the corporation on their behalf. And many social and environmental campaigners are now focusing their attentions on the laws that allow shareholders and investors the protection of their 'invisible friend'—the legal fiction that is the corporation.

> "The overwhelming majority of the tens
> of thousands of federal and state regu-
> lations that carry criminal penalties
> are aimed directly at business organi-
> zations."

Corporations Are Over-Regulated

Edwin Meese III

While many critics charge that the American judicial system is prejudiced in favor of corporations that commit white-collar crimes, Edwin Meese III, the author of the following viewpoint, argues that in reality the reverse is true. According to Meese, corporations are unfairly punished even when they come forward of their own volition to report illegal acts. Meese also claims that attorney–client privileges enjoyed by individual Americans accused of a crime rarely apply when the defendants are corporations or their chief executives.

Edwin Meese served as the seventy-fifth attorney general of the United States from 1985 to 1988. He was a contributing author to Judicial Tyranny: The New Kings of America.

Edwin Meese III, "Closing Commentary on Corporate Criminality: Legal, Ethical, and Managerial Implications," *American Criminal Law Review*, vol. 44, Fall 2007, pp. 1545–1552. Copyright © 2007 Edwin Meese III. Reproduced by permission.

As you read, consider the following questions:

1. According to the author, what is one aspect of "increased corporate criminalization"?

2. What are the three conditions that if met by a corporation should, in Meese's view, shield them from criminal prosecution?

3. What reform does the author suggest should be adopted by government to help regulate corporate offenses?

An unprecedented politicization of American criminal-law policy and practice has taken place over the past fifty years. Perhaps nowhere is this more evident today than in the area of corporate criminality. In step with this period of increasing politicization, the size and scope of criminal law enforcement, especially at the federal level, has expanded dramatically. The average business person and the average corporation have little or no hope of knowing all of the thousands of criminal-law statutes—and tens of thousands of criminal law regulations—by which they must abide in order to remain on the right side of the law. This is one of the primary reasons why it is no longer possible to avoid becoming a criminal by relying on one's conscience and general understanding of the law. A second is that state and federal lawmakers have criminalized many forms of productive economic and social activity that, until very recently, were never considered wrongful.

Many leading commentators demonstrate indifference at best toward white-collar defendants who have been subjected to unjust criminal proceedings. But in my view, corporations and other business organizations and their employees are unusually vulnerable today to heavy-handed enforcement of the criminal law. The swift demise of worldwide accounting powerhouse Arthur Andersen just days after it was indicted has communicated an unmistakable message to all corporate boards of directors: If you want your company to survive, you must do whatever the government expects of you in order to avoid an indictment, which otherwise could prove to be your death sentence. As a result, government criteria for determining whether to prosecute a business organization—criteria that were originally intended to distinguish between business organizations that are criminally corrupt and those that undertake reasonable, good faith efforts to act as responsible, law-abiding corporate citizens—have a far different effect. These criteria are routinely used to coerce (sometimes directly but more often indirectly) business organizations into waiving essential protections against unjust criminal proceedings and capitulating to harsh conditions in return for the government's agreement not to prosecute—at least temporarily.

No other class of defendants who lack the intent to engage in any wrongful conduct whatsoever is as vulnerable to conviction for the wrongs committed by others as is the class of business organizations and their directors and managers. This class has been hit the hardest by the last fifty years of judicial and legislative innovations. These innovations include bringing into the service of criminal prosecution and punishment doctrines that the common-law developed to remedy torts— where money damages have always been the historical remedy for wrongs committed. These innovative criminal law doctrines include strict criminal liability, vicarious criminal liability, and respondeat superior. Their use in service of criminal prosecutions has transformed much economically and socially beneficial conduct into act-at-your-peril activities. Even an inadvertent misstep by those acting with all due care can result in an organization suffering criminal penalties and individuals spending time in prison. And of course, the overwhelming majority of the tens of thousands of federal and state regulations that carry criminal penalties are aimed directly at business organizations and their employees. . . .

America Is Over-regulated

Criminal prosecution and punishment is the most powerful force that government regularly uses against its own citizens. Many commentators recognize that whenever the protections one class of Americans receives against unjust prosecution and punishment deteriorates, that deterioration has grave implications for the protections afforded all Americans. This is as true when the class is composed of the affluent and successful as it is when the class is composed of the socially and economically disadvantaged. Precedent shapes every aspect of our criminal justice system. . . .

America has also become a heavily over-regulated nation. One of the best scholarly estimates indicates that the number of criminal offenses created in the federal regulatory code is well over 10,000. . . . The federal government could use the criminal process to enforce as many as 300,000 federal regulations.

One aspect of this increased criminalization is the imposition of criminal penalties for many forms of economic and social activity that, until very recently, were never considered wrongful. The average American today cannot begin to imagine the range of seemingly innocent activities that could cause him or her to suffer criminal prosecution and punishment.

At the same time as the criminal law has exploded in size and scope, the traditional protections that have shielded Americans from unjust prosecution and conviction are in danger of being lost. During the twentieth century the Supreme Court arguably held in multiple cases, for example, that the Constitution does not require a criminal conviction to be supported by proof of traditional *mens rea* ["guilty mind"]. These holdings have had catastrophic consequences for American criminal law. Legislators at both the state and federal levels routinely enact criminal laws that have no meaningful mens rea requirement. Because this fundamental protection is missing, Americans who had no intention of engaging in conduct that is inherently wrongful or of violating any law are frequently punished by criminal fines and imprisonment.

For centuries, the attorney-client privilege and work-product protections have facilitated law-abiding conduct and provided a solid foundation for innocent Americans to mount a meaningful defense against wrongful prosecution. These protections promised complete confidentiality to all clients who in good faith sought legal advice from an attorney. Essayists and symposium participants have underscored how greatly corporate criminality standards threaten these long-standing protections. Their loss in the corporate context undermines not only the Sixth Amendment right to counsel but individual employees' Fifth Amendment rights against self-incrimination.

The experts ... are correct when they conclude that deferred prosecution agreements and non-prosecution agreements for corporations under criminal investigation often amount to little more than coerced settlements. The potential for a corporation to suffer devastating and irreparable harm from its mere indictment, as happened with Arthur Andersen, is so grave that it inevitably multiplies the likelihood of coerced settlements. Former Deputy Attorney General George Terwilliger has stated that all good lawyers must often advise corporations that they cannot afford to contest a prosecution at trial, regardless of how unfounded the charges may be. Instead they must work out a settlement with the government that usually includes a plea of guilty. . . .

Restoration of Integrity

So what are the answers? Where do we go from here? Several of the experts have suggested promising reforms, and they have also provided sound guidance for choosing among competing proposals. When considering possible reforms, we ought to look first at purpose: What is the purpose of law enforcement with respect to corporations? Obviously it is to

Is Too Much Oversight Bad?

The Committee on Capital Markets Regulation concluded that increased oversight by regulators and prosecutors in the five years since the Enron scandal has put U.S. financial markets at a competitive disadvantage. The panel ... called on authorities to restore a "proper balance" between the rules' costs and benefits.

Business leaders increasingly have expressed concern that the United States is losing ground in the form of corporate stock listings to more lightly regulated foreign exchanges in London and elsewhere because of burdensome rules and expensive private lawsuits. Investor advocates attribute the move abroad to a series of unrelated reasons, including the increasing globalization of business and steep underwriting fees charged by U.S. investment banks.

Carrie Johnson,
Washington Post, *November 30, 2006.*

gain compliance—compliance with the law, compliance with those statutes that are providing for the public safety. The enforcement of criminal law against corporations is similarly focused on preventing and punishing fraud. Allegations of fraud have been at the heart of many of the large corporate cases that we have seen recently. Therefore, both the policies and the practices of the Department of Justice and the federal government should be designed to achieve these objectives: compliance, public safety, the prevention and punishment of fraud, and good corporate conduct.

With compliance as the goal, it is imperative that corporations not be penalized for doing the right thing. Many experts have pointed out that there should be a clear reward for good conduct. When, for example, a corporation has:

- developed an adequate compliance program that fulfills all reasonable requirements,

- taken all steps that are reasonably necessary to ensure employees are implementing that program, and

- conducted its own internal investigations to ferret out evidence of any wrongdoing, then (and at the very least) the material that the corporation and its counsel gathers through those investigations should not be taken by the government and used to prosecute the corporation.

Similarly, where the corporation itself initiates the contact with the Department of Justice, discloses information of possible wrongdoing, and seeks the government's advice on how to proceed, the Department should not turn around and prosecute that corporation using information that the government would not have received but for the corporation's or its attorneys' voluntary disclosure. Yet this is exactly what happens in some cases. Taking reasonable steps to investigate possible wrongdoing and to correct and remedy any substantiated wrongdoing is an act of good corporate citizenship. It should be rewarded. These steps, and the information the corporation collects in the course of taking them, should not be utilized as a basis for going forward with a prosecution.

Some experts have suggested that there should be a formal presumption against criminal prosecution whenever these various elements of good corporate conduct are present. Rather than criminal prosecution, the recognized norm should be either a civil action undertaken by parties who allegedly suffered actual harm from the wrongdoing or some form of administrative or regulatory enforcement proceedings. . . .

Fixing the Broken System

A number of suggestions have been made for specific action by legislatures or by the Department of Justice. One such idea involves comprehensive reform of the federal criminal code. But the record of similar efforts in the past shows the difficulty of achieving such reform. During the 1970s, a commission was appointed to undertake comprehensive reform of the federal criminal code. This effort was led by Edmund G. Brown, former governor of California, who had been a district attorney and state attorney general. Brown and his group worked very hard to accomplish that goal, but their effort did not result in substantial change in the law. Mixing the policy and the process of code reform has been the death knell of similar movements in the past. If policy changes are to be recommended, the reform team should separately provide to Congress the proposals and let that body determine their disposition. The revised code itself must be neutrally reorganized so that the policy changes do not get so mixed up with the process, that real criminal code reform is rejected.

One institutional and procedural reform that should be adopted by both the House and the Senate would cause both judiciary committees to take a far more active role in overseeing every legislative proposal that adds or changes criminal offenses or penalties. This might require the adoption of new rules—or strict enforcement of existing rules—granting judiciary committees ultimate jurisdiction over all proposed legislation that would change the criminal law. Members of the judiciary committees should take a more active role in overseeing proposed changes to criminal provisions and penalties. The leadership of both houses of Congress as well will need to be persuaded of how essential this process is to restoring a fair and effective criminal justice system.

One reform that should be implemented is to eliminate Congress's practice of allowing regulatory agencies in the executive branch to attach criminal penalties to regulations they

issue where the precise offense is not spelled out in the underlying statute. If a matter is important enough to label someone a criminal and send him to prison, then it ought to be
important enough for Congress itself to consider whether a
particular course of conduct is worthy of a prison term. We
should not have thousands of new criminal penalties attached
to regulations without congressional scrutiny.

The suggestion of an affirmative defense against conviction for corporations who have operated in good faith is an
excellent idea. Obviously alternatives to criminal prosecution
already exist through civil litigation and administrative action.
These alternatives would allow the government to reserve the
hammer of criminal prosecution for those few cases in which
it is truly warranted because of the severity and intentionality
of the corporation's wrongdoing.

Finally, the idea of corporate restorative justice is an appropriate means of handling many violations. Rather than going through the entire litigation process, restorative justice
would give credit for actions that are taken by the corporation
to restore matters to the state they would have been in but for
the wrongdoing. This would preserve and enhance the rem-
edies available for those who may have been harmed while
avoiding the problems necessarily inherent in the criminal
process when it is applied to corporations.

> *"Corporations have a well-earned reputation for capturing regulatory agencies, undoing legal restrictions, and otherwise meddling in their own future."*

Corporations Need Regulatory Restraints

Ted Nace

Ted Nace, the author of the following viewpoint, argues that criminal or unethical behavior is endemic to corporations by their nature. Despite masquerading as beneficial entities in the public trust, corporations are modern viruses that over the years have steadily improved their abilities to evade legal consequences for their activities. Citing the case of the Dodge v. Ford Motor Corp. as an example, Nace suggests that courts have traditionally ruled in favor of corporate interests at the consumer's expense.

Ted Nace is a writer and the former staff director of the Dakota Research Council.

As you read, consider the following questions:

1. What are two of the ways the author claims that Exxon-Mobil sets itself apart policy-wise from rival oil companies?

2. What are several of the methods Nace advises implementing to constrain corporate power?

3. In the author's opinion, what are the two benefits of viewing the corporation as a dynamic technology?

Above the stage is the glowing logo of the corporation, and next to the logo, in a touch of exquisite irony, a glistening blue image of Planet Earth hangs in midair as though floating through space.

It is a piece of choreography disguised as a democratic proceeding: the annual meeting of a Fortune 500 corporation. To the right of [chairman and CEO of ExxonMobil Corporation Lee] Raymond sits a group of seven men and three women. Their role appears to be the opposite of that of the chorus in a Greek play: to be seen, but not to make a sound. They are the nominees for the board of directors, each hand-picked by management. Everything is preordained, except that there seems to be a small fly in the ointment. A party pooper.

In the aisle to my left a well-dressed woman approaches a freestanding microphone. This is the portion of the meeting during which stockholders are allowed to present statements for or against resolutions that have been proposed for a vote. The woman's voice is soft but firm, "Mr. Chairman, on behalf of the members of the Sisters of St. Dominic and the Capuchin Order of the Roman Catholic Church, I wish to argue in support of Resolution 8 tying the compensation of management to certain indices of environmental and social performance by the company—."

For a heartbeat, the lock-step march of the meeting seems in jeopardy.

"Whatever you have to say," cuts in the chairman, "the matter has already been decided in the negative by proxies received prior to this meeting. You have one minute forty seconds."

"Mr. Chairman, you have the power to restrict this debate, but your authority is not legitimate. I represent twenty thousand nuns and clergy who have an ownership stake in this company. Their pensions depend on its financial results, but at the same time they wish to see financial performance balanced against other factors, including the urgent need to protect the environment and to safeguard human rights."

"You have fifty-five seconds remaining."

Speaker after speaker approaches the microphones to make statements on behalf of a variety of resolutions to reform the company. One asks for a policy forbidding discrimination against gays and lesbians. Another proposes that ExxonMobil alter its stance on global warming. Yet another opposes drilling in the Arctic National Wildlife Refuge.

The most startling of the proposals requests that Exxon-Mobil end its involvement in the Indonesian province of Aceh, where the company maintains a close relationship with military forces that have been ruthlessly suppressing a local separatist movement. According to a lawsuit filed in federal court by the International Labor Rights Fund, ExxonMobil provided buildings used by the Indonesian military to torture local activists, and its bulldozers dug the mass graves used to bury the victims. There will be no real debate on any of these matters. The atmosphere is oppressive, even intimidating. Security guards stand ready to forcibly eject from the hall any speaker who deliberately exceeds the meager time limits.

The New Dictators

Of course, if this were a small family business, no one would expect nuns, environmentalists, and human rights activists to have any say over its dealings, nor would the public be interested. But according to the glossy materials in my hand, ExxonMobil represents the reunification of two of the thirty-four strands of John D. Rockefeller's Standard Oil empire: Standard Oil of New York (renamed Mobil in 1966) and Standard Oil of New Jersey (renamed Exxon in 1972). Its total revenues now exceed $200 billion annually. This is not a business, it is a world power. Its operations affect not only its tens of thousands of employees and millions of customers, but large areas of the planet. On a strictly dollar-for-dollar basis, the revenues of ExxonMobil exceed the governmental budgets of all but seven of the world's nations.

The man at the podium commands a private domain. That he conducts himself like a dictator is no accident. In fact, his power actually exceeds that of most dictators. Around the world, they are more likely to hurry to answer his phone calls than he would be to answer theirs.

As I watch this larger-than-life executive assert his power, I reflect on the notion that the corporation is a nobody—an entity divorced from human values or designs. That notion would seem to be belied by the very real somebody who is running this meeting, this human being named Lee Raymond, whose political views clearly drive this corporation and its policies. Thanks to Mr. Raymond, ExxonMobil has set itself apart. For example, on global warming, most of the other oil giants have taken a different stance. They have announced that they agree with the science that has forecast global warming and that they endorse the Kyoto Protocols on global warming. Competitors like British Petroleum (the largest maker of photovoltaic cells) and Royal Dutch/Shell (one of the biggest developers of wind farms) are racing to anticipate and ride the trend toward renewable sources of energy. Similarly, not every company opposes gay rights, as ExxonMobil does. Numerous corporations, seeking to retain talented staff, provide health benefits to domestic partners.

These policy differences among oil companies would seem to belie the notion of corporations as mindless, impersonal entities. Clearly, policy is in the hands of human beings, each free to adopt a wide scope in their tactics and strategies. Still, I would argue that this freedom is constrained. Let's imagine, for a moment, that the night before the meeting Lee Raymond had been visited by a series of Dickensian ghosts, who had rattled their chains and urged him for the sake of his grandchildren's lives and his own eternal soul to sacrifice a hefty share of ExxonMobil's profits in order to take the company on a radically divergent path toward social justice and environmental protection. At the annual meeting, Raymond—a young grandchild in each arm—had announced his intention of moving the company in the new direction, making a passionate speech about human rights and the fate of the planet.

What would have happened next? It is predictable enough. Either (a) Raymond's board of directors would have fired him posthaste, or (b) both Raymond and the board would soon have been staring down the barrel of a class-action shareholder lawsuit charging them with violating their legally mandated fiduciary responsibility toward the owners of the company.

A Corporation's Sole Responsibility

In fact, that's exactly what happened to none other than Henry Ford, who wanted to plough his company's retained earnings into building more factories, in order to "employ still more men, to spread the benefits of this industrial system to the greatest possible number, to help them build up their lives and their homes." Unfortunately for Ford, his shareholders took him to court, demanding that the company's retained earnings be distributed as dividends. Even though Henry Ford had pioneered the assembly line, the Michigan Supreme Court ruled bluntly in 1919 in *Dodge v. Ford Motor Co.* that he could

"Time, temperature, and corporate ethics readings." Cartoon by Harley Schwadron. www.CartoonStock.com.

not devote the company he had created to his personal goal of creating as many factory jobs as possible, if doing so would reduce the profits of the company. Profits, said the court, were the only goal that Ford was allowed to pursue:

> A business corporation is organized and carried on primarily for the profit of the stockholders. The powers of the directors are to be employed for that end. The discretion of directors is to be exercised in the choice of means to attain that end, and does not extend to a change in the end itself, to reduction of profits, or to the nondistribution of profits among stockholders in order to devote them to other purposes.

Since Ford defended his plan of reinvestment in terms of social goals rather than in terms of maximizing shareholder returns, he lost the case.

Americans have always been fascinated by the personalities of business tycoons. But if we really want to understand what it would take to put corporations on a more socially healthy course, we have to look past the personalities and opinions of the human beings who manage these institutions. In truth, the power yielded by Lee Raymond has little to do with the man himself. CEOs will come and go, while ExxonMobil, this immense, morphing, shapeless entity, lives on. It is the company's power, not Raymond's intellect or force of will, that causes presidents and dictators to pick up the phone. . . .

"Divine Right"

At one time, the institution known as the state seemed similarly impregnable. Prior to the late eighteenth century, virtually all cultures were organized as monolithic top-down power structures enforced by monopolies of overt violence and by ideologies such as the "divine right of kings" that taught subservience and compliance. One way of thinking about the American Revolution is to see it as a reengineering of the state. Like a computer programmer debugging a piece of software, the framers of the American system rolled up their sleeves, tweaked this and that, and came up with a new design.

One can see this practical bent in *The Federalist Papers*, where Alexander Hamilton writes about society like a mechanic considering different bolts and screws:

> The science of politics, like most other sciences, has received great improvement. The efficacy of various principles is now well understood, which were either not known at all, or imperfectly known to the ancients. The regular distribution of power into distinct departments; the introduction of legislative balances and checks; the institution of courts composed of judges, holding their offices during good behavior; the representation of the people in the legislature, by deputies of their own election; these are either wholly new discoveries,

or have made their principal progress towards perfection in modern times. They are means, and powerful means, by which the excellencies of republican government may be retained, and its imperfections lessened or avoided.

Social change, according to this vision of things, isn't just a matter of asserting values. It's also a matter of innovating and implementing specific ways for realizing those values, mechanisms like democratic selection of leaders, separation of powers, human rights, and judicial review.

For example, the concept of human rights can be seen as a safety feature—an organizational airbag that helps prevent large, powerful institutions from crushing vulnerable human beings. To make any such design feature work, it must be accompanied by legal systems to interpret it and police power to enforce it.

As new design ideas for the state were implemented in America and elsewhere, it became apparent that some worked better than others. For example, compare the American experience with that of the French in crafting a working system of human rights. Although France's Declaration of the Rights of Man and the Citizen is more extensive than America's Bill of Rights, the two countries diverged in mechanisms for enforcement. In France, enforcement was placed in the hands of the National Assembly and its representatives on the Committee for Public Safety. In America, Chief Justice [John] Marshall's assertion of Supreme Court authority in *Marbury v. Madison* (1803) established judicial review in a separate branch of government. In France, the human rights system quickly broke down; in the United States it worked, however imperfectly. International human rights expert Geoffrey Robertson attributes the difference to the fact that *Marbury v. Madison* "provided human rights in the U.S. with a set of teeth, by endorsing courts rather than legislatures as their enforcement mechanism."

Just as it was necessary to innovate and implement specific new features in order to democratize and constrain state power, the same applies to corporate power. A short list of changes might include the following: (1) revoking the doctrine of corporate constitutional rights; (2) curbing corporate quasi-rights as appropriate—for example, requiring corporations to renew their charters every five years; (3) banning corporations from political activity; (4) shoring up the boundaries of "noncorporate" spaces in society—for example, prohibiting advertising aimed at children; (5) expanding the scope of worker and customer rights vis-à-vis corporations; (6) strengthening countervailing institutions, especially unions; and (7) promoting noncorporate institutions like public schools and economic forms like municipal utilities, family farms, consumer cooperatives, and employee-run enterprises.

Modern-Day Monsters

Of course, the notion that we might simply decide on some design changes and then implement them, as though corporate power were a malfunctioning carburetor that needed some new seals and valves, is disingenuous. Unlike car parts, corporations are not passive objects. They're run by smart, resourceful people, who can be expected to defend their power. When you fix the carburetor on your car, the carburetor does not start thinking about how to undo the fix. This makes the problem of corporate power different from more routine problems. As the history of the late nineteenth century shows, corporations are veritable Houdinis in their capacity to slip out of legally imposed strictures. Corporate power is like a germ that develops a resistance to the newest antibiotic, like the mouse that learns to steal the cheese from the trap, like the recidivist who gets out of prison and then commits another crime. Corporations have a well-earned reputation for capturing regulatory agencies, undoing legal restrictions, and otherwise meddling in their own future. . . .

If we look at the corporation like a naturalist studying a new life form, we see that it has an evolutionary history, a characteristic structure, a set of behaviors. The genius of the corporation is the simplicity, flexibility, and modularity of its design. It scales to any size, serves virtually any function, adapts to any culture, and is robust—capable, at least in principle, of functioning indefinitely. It is programmed to survive, to maintain its structure and functional integrity, to grow, to avoid danger and recover from damage, to adapt, and to respond to the outside world.

There is nothing malicious or even conscious about the tendency of the corporation to seek power. The process is slow and incremental; the world is bent in tiny steps. But over time, such small acts result in the wholesale transformation of society.

Does that sound far-fetched? If so, consider the changes that propelled the conversion of the corporation from its legally restrained status prior to the Civil War to a liberated and empowered one at the end of the nineteenth century. Next, trace the trend of empowerment through the twentieth century, to nation-sized, politically aggressive corporations such as ExxonMobil. Finally, extrapolate the trend another century or two, as corporations continue to tinker with and alter the constraining web of laws that define their power, as they seek to overcome problems, eliminate threats, or achieve goals.

The notion of creating a technology so dynamic and life-like that it becomes dangerous to ourselves has been a theme in the modern mind since 1818, when Mary Shelly's novel *Frankenstein* transposed the medieval legend of the golem— the creature composed of clay and animated by kabalistic incantations and procedures—to the industrial age. In general, such tales paint visions of horror and tragedy. The horror has to do with powerful life forces escaping the normalizing checks of nature. The tragedy has to do with the notion that in humans the talent for creating such trouble exceeds the capacity to prevent or manage it.

Expanding Sphere of Influence

Because it is so adaptable, the corporation seems on an inexorable course toward permeating every aspect of life, not just the traditional economic spheres but increasingly such public spheres as schools and prisons, and such personal spheres as preparing meals and entertaining children. In many ways the corporation is coming to know us better than we know it. It involves itself with us intimately. It participates in our birthing, our education, even our sexuality; it tracks our personal habits, entertains us, imprisons us; it helps us fight off dread diseases, manufactures the food products that we eat, barters and trades with us in a common economic system, jostles us in the political arena, talks to us in a human voice, sues us if we threaten it.

In recent years, scientists have speculated about the potential of various existing or future technologies to veer out of human control. Nuclear power, genetic engineering, artificial intelligence, and the microscale engineering known as nanotechnology have all been the subject of such concerns, however theoretical. Writing in *Wired* magazine, computer scientist Bill Joy warned about the trajectory of research on nanotechnology, describing a nightmare scenario in which an artificially created micro-organism, lacking any natural predators but capable of reproducing itself and metabolizing any sort of living substance, spreads out of control through the biosphere, reducing everything in its path to "grey goo."

It is time for those who worry about runaway technologies to include the corporation among the objects of their concern. In this case, the invention is not a new one or a futuristic one. The experiment is taking place all around us. The laboratory is the world. . . .

A Matter of Control

So where is the grey goo? I just looked out my window, and I saw the sky, some trees, a rooftop. If our world is being chewed up by a swarm of organizational locusts, the process must be rather slow and quiet. Of course, that's exactly the point that the environmental movement has been making now for decades, and their concerns about global warming, species extinction, and general environmental degradation are based on fact, not speculation. The sky may not literally be falling, but it's filling up with greenhouse gases, and the rest of the biosphere is under continual assault. Again and again, when people organize to find political solutions to such problems, the chief obstacle blocking their way is the opposing political muscle of corporations like ExxonMobil.

There are two benefits to seeing the corporation as a technology, and a dynamic one at that. First, this recognition quickly reorganizes the question of whether corporations deserve rights. Rather than what *rights* corporations deserve, the question is reversed: What sort of *restraints* will prevent runaway corporate power? The basic approach is suggested by Isaac Asimov's "Three Laws of Robotics":

1. A robot may not injure a human being, or, through inaction, allow a human being to come to harm.

2. A robot must obey the orders given it by human beings except where such orders would conflict with the First Law.

3. A robot must protect its own existence as long as protection does not conflict with the First or Second Laws.

Obviously, a democratic society can't control corporate power by means of three simple rules. Nevertheless, Asimov's point is exactly right: either we control our creations, or they control us. There is no middle ground. Giving corporations constitutional rights does the exact opposite of what is needed. Rather than being prevented on constitutional grounds from implementing laws such as campaign finance reform, legislators need a free hand in creating a legal framework that can hold corporate power in check.

The second benefit to seeing the corporation as a dynamic technology—as a quasi-living thing—is that it allows us to place corporations into a familiar category of problem. Humans have a long and deep experience with the shaping and softening process known as "domestication," in which the useful qualities of a species are fostered while the dangerous ones are pruned away. The work of domesticating the corporation can't be accomplished with a single piece of legislation, and it's not even realistic to think it can happen in a single generation. It will involve a great deal of legislation, including constitutional change. It will involve the evolution of a clearer vision that *rights* are a human privilege, not an institutional one. It will involve the end of the notion that powerful organizations ought to enjoy indefinite terms of existence. It will require broadening the notion of human rights to incorporate the various forms of interaction between humans and corporations—as consumers, as workers, or in other contexts. It will require clear boundaries and firewalls that maintain politics as a "humans-only" space. It will require similarly clear definitions of other humans-only spaces: the family, education, and so on. Finally, and most importantly, it will require a deep change in attitude, an embedded skepticism. The corporation is a powerful tool, and that makes it a dangerous one. After we domesticate and democratize it—assuming we manage to do so—we'll still have to warn our kids: "Watch out. Keep an eye on this thing. And don't ever forget: it can bite."

> *"The origin of the 'white-collar crime'*
> *concept derives from a socialist, anti-*
> *business viewpoint that defines the term*
> *by the class of those it stigmatizes."*

Definitions of White-Collar Crime Are Unfair to Business

John S. Baker, Jr.

John S. Baker, Jr., the author of the following viewpoint, claims that the most underreported victims of white-collar crimes are corporations. In Baker's view, associating "white-collar" criminals with businessmen unfairly holds the wealthy to a different legal standard, punishing them, in effect, for being prosperous, while many middle-class Americans are guilty of what legally constitute white-collar crimes on a daily basis but who are not prosecuted. According to Baker, the phrase "white-collar crime" originally fostered a socialist, anticorporate bias that irrationally persists in the minds of legislators and the public perception to this day.

John S. Baker, Jr., is Dale E. Bennett Professor of Law at the Louisiana State University Law Center.

John S. Baker, Jr., "The Sociological Origins of White Collar Crime, Legal Memorandum #14," *Heritage Foundation*, www.heritage.org, October 4, 2004. Reproduced by permission.

As you read, consider the following questions:

1. According to the author, what are two examples of "white-collar crime" committed by middle-class Americans that generally go unprosecuted?

2. Who coined the term "white-collar crime" as cited by Baker?

3. In the author's opinion, what is the "essential element of crime" ignored by Edwin Sutherland?

A re millions of middle-class Americans really white-collar criminals? The unauthorized importation of prescription drugs from a foreign country is a federal crime. So is "sharing" copyrighted material without permission. Assisting someone in the commission of a federal crime is also a federal crime. Countless American seniors purchase prescription drugs from Mexican and Canadian pharmacies. Millions of Americans, including teens using family computers, share copyrighted music without paying for it.

According to the Department of Justice, "White-collar offenses shall constitute those classes of non-violent illegal activities which principally involve traditional notions of deceit, deception, concealment, manipulation, breach of trust, subterfuge or illegal circumvention." Under that definition, the illegal purchase of prescriptions and music pirating clearly qualify. The Justice Department has recently promoted the idea that enforcement of federal crimes should be uniform. Nevertheless, it is highly unlikely that federal prosecutors will hand down millions (or any) indictments of seniors, parents, and children for these crimes.

Despite the rhetoric, the decision to prosecute is unavoidably discretionary. How do prosecutors determine whom to prosecute? All too often, the choice reflects contemporary politics—and today's criminal du jour is the "white-collar" crook. Yet when most people talk about vigorously prosecuting white-collar crime, they don't mean locking up those who purchase medicine from neighboring countries or pirate music over the Internet, despite the fact that such crimes defraud pharmaceutical and music corporations (and thus their shareholders) of billions of dollars.

What accounts for the difference in treatment? The Justice Department's formal definition of white-collar crime disregards class or economic status. But the truth is that in white-collar cases, such distinctions do influence decisions about whether or not to prosecute. Government prosecutors are far more likely to indict the "upper-class" businessman who works for Tyco—or the faceless Arthur Andersen partnership—than a middle-class grandmother who buys medications in Canada. This reflects the socialist origin of the "white-collar crime" concept. The war against white-collar crime thus unwittingly stems from and embraces a class-based sociological concept of crime.

Remaking the Definition of Crime

The terms "white-collar crime" and its offshoot, "organized crime," reflect a half-century-old movement to remake the very definition of crime. Professor Edwin Sutherland, a sociologist who coined the term "white-collar crime," disagreed with certain basic substantive and procedural principles of criminal law. In his landmark book, *White Collar Crime*, first published in 1949, Sutherland dismisses the traditional *mens rea* (criminal intent) requirement and the presumption of innocence. He suggests that the "rules of criminal intent and presumption of innocence . . . are not required in all prosecution in criminal courts and the number of exceptions authorized by statutes is increasing." If nothing else, his disregard for age-old foundational principles of criminal law should cast doubt on the balance of Sutherland's work.

Sutherland goes on to construct a class-based definition of "white-collar crime." He is concerned with who the alleged perpetrator was, rather than what that person might have done. "White collar crime," says Sutherland, is "crime committed by a person of respectability and high social status in the course of his occupation." With this radical redefinition, Sutherland attempted to drain the word "crime" of its meaning. He made distinctions not on the basis of an act or intent, but according to the status of the accused. . . .

A Presumption of Guilt

Sutherland relies on the claim that both corporate and individual defendants are routinely deprived of the presumption of innocence in criminal proceedings. His corporate examples, however, are nearly all civil and regulatory cases rather than actual criminal prosecutions. Sutherland, perhaps due to a lack of any substantive legal education, conflates all enforcement activity against businesses (such as civil suits and settlement agreements) with criminal prosecution—even where no crime was ever committed. To Sutherland, proof of corporate culpability is unimportant. He justifies his mislabeling by alleging that the powerful—despite the lack of criminal procedure protection that he recognizes and celebrates—receive preferential treatment in the legal system.

Sutherland's updated 1983 treatise on white-collar crime explains:

> The thesis of this book, stated positively, is that persons of the upper socioeconomic class engage in much criminal behavior; that this criminal behavior differs from the criminal behavior of the lower socioeconomic class principally in the administrative procedures which are used in dealing with the offenders; and that variations in administrative procedures are not significant from the point of view of causation of crime. . . .

> [M]any of the defendants in usual criminal cases, being in relative poverty, do not get good defense and consequently secure little benefit from these rules; on the other hand, the commissions [that enforce certain commercial regulations]

come close to observing these rules of proof and evidence although they are not required to do so.

Sutherland intended to provide a basis for facilitating more convictions of executives and corporations by reconceptualizing crime through the term "white-collar crime." He began by equating the "adverse decisions" of regulatory agencies with criminal convictions. As to people involved in business, Sutherland sought to deemphasize the presumption of innocence and the mens rea requirement to facilitate establishing their criminal liability. Yet what Professor Sutherland called a crime was often only a regulatory violation. Intent is not normally considered in such enforcement actions; thus many of Sutherland's "crimes" may have been inadvertent, unintended acts. Nevertheless, Sutherland was determined to classify such acts as crimes.

Sutherland's influence is clearly evident in the contemporary substance and practice of federal criminal law. Many federal offenses prosecuted under the label of "white-collar crime" are regulatory or public welfare offenses, rather than true crimes. The principal architect of the U.S. Sentencing Commission's guidelines for sentencing organizations cites Professor Sutherland's "social science research," among that of others, to explain the need for the guidelines, namely the "evidence of preferential treatment for white collar offenders."

Stigma Without Sin

Often, when convinced that a person or class of persons is guilty of a crime, people become impatient with legal niceties. Sutherland and others who assume the guilt of much of the business world believe that the ordinary protections of the law need not apply to persons involved in business. When such attempts at pre-judgment are directed at any other group—even at terrorists—civil libertarians cry "tyranny." Yet, a civil libertarian outcry in defense of corporate defendants appears most unlikely. Concluding that those engaged in business do not

Types of White Collar Crime

- Embezzlement - the taking of someone's property by a person with whom it is entrusted.

- Bribery - occurs when someone gives or takes a bribe.

- Larceny - involves taking someone's property without paying for or returning it.

- Extortion - also known as blackmail.

- Fraud - this often includes but is not limited to health care fraud and tax fraud.

- Price Fixing - an agreement between two parties to set prices for a certain product, thereby violating free market operations.

- Racketeering - the extortion of money by force or a pattern of criminal activity committed to further the interests of a criminal syndicate.

- Computer Fraud - using a computer to commit a crime.

- Obstruction of Justice - interfering with the criminal process by impeding an investigation.

- Perjury - lying while under oath in a judicial proceeding.

- Securities and Commodities Law Violations

- Environmental Law Violations

LawyerShop, 2008. www.lawyershop.com.

deserve the presumption of innocence, Professor Sutherland dispensed with the essential (and often most difficult to prove) element of crime: a guilty mind. Although it would be unconstitutional to eliminate the presumption of innocence, Sutherland tries to circumvent this by eliminating the mental element requirement.

Sutherland dismissed the most fundamental principles of criminal law in pursuing his belief that the law unfairly stigmatizes the poor, while it does not stigmatize the rich and powerful enough. Claiming that the law should treat the two classes more equally, he wrote:

> Seventy five percent of the persons committed to state prisons are probably not, aside from their unesteemed cultural attainments, "criminals in the usual sense of the word." It may be excellent policy to eliminate the stigma of crime from violations of law by both the upper and the lower classes, but we are not here concerned with policy.

Sutherland did not seek to eliminate the stigma of crime (although dispensing with the intent requirement should theoretically achieve this goal). Rather, he sought to expand it. The concept of "white-collar crime" has ensured that, in the quest for greater egalitarianism, the stigma of crime has been applied against much of corporate America. But before society stigmatizes and punishes a criminal defendant, the rule of law requires that reliable procedures determine the defendant's culpability. Although some academics might wish it were so, it is not a crime to be wealthy or powerful.

By disregarding culpability, Sutherland sought to apply the stigma usually associated with criminal convictions to businesspeople and corporations in non-criminal regulatory proceedings. His book charged that "70 corporations [discussed in his book] committed crimes according to 779 adverse decisions [although] the criminality of their behavior was . . . blurred and concealed by special procedures." In Sutherland's view, the complexity of business transactions may make it more difficult to prove criminal activity. But it is equally possible that complexity was evidence that in a particular case no criminal conduct occurred. Without requiring proof beyond a reasonable doubt of a clearly stated criminal intent, there is no basis for distinguishing guilty from innocent actions. When prosecutors indict corporations or their executives for federal crimes, relaxed standards for proving criminal intent result in convictions where actual innocence has been "blurred and concealed."

Traditionally, and for good reason, the stigma of crime attaches only to individuals proven to have been "morally culpable" by virtue of having acted with a guilty state of mind. In Sutherland's view, this traditional protection is an antiquated technicality. Rather, culpability should involve an externalized standard of whether a defendant's acts violated the "moral sentiments" of the people. Of course, as the Supreme Court has forcefully stated, the most basic "moral sentiment" is that society not stigmatize persons as criminals unless they are proven to have a guilty mind. . . .

Sociological Echoes

Sutherland and his successors greatly expanded the scope of crime by shifting the focus to corporations and individuals in the upper socioeconomic classes. A lawyer-sociologist critic of Sutherland's work, Paul W. Tappan, long ago noted that Sutherland's definition of crime departed from the legal definition. Tappan charged that this development was a "seductive movement to revolutionize the concepts of crime and [the] criminal. . . ." According to Tappan, Professor Sutherland's definition of "white-collar crime" includes "a boor, a sinner, a moral leper or the devil incarnate but he does not become a criminal through sociological name-calling."

The term "white-collar crime" has expanded even further, to include such an array of crime that it has become too amorphous for analysis. Some sociologists, finding even Sutherland's very loose definition "too restrictive," "have dropped the class of the offender as a relevant element." Thus, "white-collar" crime has now become a division of organizational crime. One example is the Justice Department effort to force corporations to waive their privilege against self-incrimination as a condition of pleading guilty. This nascent trend is consistent with and sociologically derived from Sutherland's thesis that "white-collar" criminals are not entitled to the same constitutional protections afforded other defendants. Recently and rather remarkably, the Justice Department has espoused an essentially class-based view of the law in requesting that the Sentencing Commission disallow departures from the sentencing guidelines for "white collar criminal defendants, who typically have sophisticated counsel."

In short, Sutherland's influence continues to this day. Indeed, compared to contemporary theoreticians Sutherland might seem to have been a veritable cheerleader for corporate America. Although mentored by a protégé of socialist Thorstein Veblen, Sutherland "fundamentally was an advocate of free enterprise," albeit a highly regulated form thereof. At the conclusion of his book, he said that the upper class commit many crimes, but he could not say whether "the upper class is more criminal or less criminal than the lower class, for the evidence is not sufficiently precise to justify comparisons and common standards and definitions are not available."

By contrast and despite a lack of evidence, Sutherland's own protégé, Donald Cressey, has repeatedly preached to college students in his standard college text on Criminology that "the people of the business world are probably more criminalistic than the people of the slums." Cressey's views are influential. He was instrumental in the creation of the "enterprise" concept, at the core of the Racketeer Influenced Corrupt Organizations Act (RICO). Supposedly designed to target "organized crime," prosecutors have used this statute to indict all kinds of corporations, and private parties have used it to sue most major corporations as well as the Catholic Church.

All have been labeled "organized criminals." And thus, Sutherland's legacy continues to echo today.

The origin of the "white-collar crime" concept derives from a socialist, anti-business viewpoint that defines the term by the class of those it stigmatizes. In coining the phrase, Sutherland initiated a political movement within the legal system. This meddling in the law perverts the justice system into a mere tool for achieving narrow political ends. As the movement expands today, those who champion it would be wise to recall its origins. For those origins reflect contemporary misuses made of criminal law—the criminalization of productive social and economic conduct, not because of its wrongful nature but, ultimately, because of fidelity to a long-discredited class-based view of society.

Periodical Bibliography

Joseph Audal, Quincy Lu, and Peter Roman — "Computer Crimes," *American Criminal Law Review*, Spring 2008.

Annette D. Beresford, Christian Desilets, Sandra Haantz, John Kane, and April Wall — "Intellectual Property and White-Collar Crime," *Trends in Organized Crime*, Summer 2005.

Thomas A. Buckhoff and Levon E. Wilson — "Ethical Lessons for Accountants," *The CPA Journal*, November 2008.

Thomas A. Hagemann — "Prosecuting Nonhuman Corporations in a Human System," *Texas Lawyer*, January 5, 2004.

Lynn Koch — "White-Collar Crime: Scandals, Schemes and Shenanigans," *Fulton County (GA) Daily Report*, August 16, 2004.

Abbe David Lowell and Kathryn C. Arnold — "Corporate Crime After 2000: A New Law Enforcement Challenge or Déjà Vu?" *American Criminal Law Review*, Spring 2003.

Russell Mokhiber — "20 Things About Corporate Crime," *Multinational Monitor*, January-February 2007.

Heather Morton — "Identity Thieves: Let's Catch Them If We Can," *State Legislatures*, January 2004.

C. Evan Stewart — "Innocent Mistakes Are Not Criminal," *American Banker*, June 24, 2005.

Emma de Vita — "White-Collar Crime: The Inside Story," *Management Today*, April 1, 2006.

John Williams — "Crime and Fear of Crime," *Sociology Review*, April 2005.

Who Commits White-Collar Crime?

Chapter Preface

When sociologist Edwin Sutherland first coined the phrase "white-collar crime," he was referring to the social status of the criminal. Since people of wealth had greater access to the finances necessary to commit such crimes in the first place, it stood to reason that only swindlers and fraudsters of a high income bracket could technically be considered white-collar criminals.

Today, however, white-collar crimes are committed over computers and wireless networks by individuals with no resources other than an Internet connection. At the other extreme, entire corporations with hundreds or even thousands of employees might be performing myriad crimes on a daily basis, unknowingly in some cases. What drives any person, let alone one who is financially secure, reasonably intelligent, and even ethical in other areas of life, to rob (usually faceless) strangers? Is it a matter of pure greed? A form of insanity? Some experts suggest that white-collar criminals are simply a natural outgrowth of an increasingly competitive and volatile marketplace who are driven by desperation or a compulsion to dominate others.

Notably, many white-collar criminals when confronted, especially those in the public eye, and asked to account for their misdeeds often claim that they never considered the legality of their actions, even after being convicted. Or they consider such questions merely impolite intrusions. In 2002, when CBS News anchor Jane Clayson interviewed style maven Martha Stewart regarding the charges of insider trading for which she would soon be indicted, Ms. Stewart, who was briskly chopping cabbage, famously replied, "I just want to focus on my salad."

The viewpoints in the following chapter offer contrasting glimpses of what makes white-collar criminals break the law, from the small-time tax evader to the predatory CEO.

Whether acting out of greed, fear, megalomania, or simply for the thrill of it, white-collar criminals share one trait in common: they never expected to get caught.

> *"There's an intrinsic link between embezzling, on one hand, and marital infidelity, public drunkenness, traffic tickets, fighting, vandalism and not paying one's personal bills, on the other."*

White-Collar Crime Is Committed by Inherently Dishonest People

Linda Wasmer Andrews

Is blaming the corporate culture for white-collar crime giving intellectually dishonest people a free pass? In the following viewpoint, author Linda Wasmer Andrews argues that this is the case. Andrews notes that independent studies appear to confirm that people who cheat and lie in their personal lives tend to be equally unreliable in their business affairs. While she agrees that the personal lives of employees are not necessarily a company's business, how a prospective employee conducts him- or herself in a nonwork setting usually suggests how he or she will behave in the workplace.

Linda Wasmer Andrews is a writer in Albuquerque, New Mexico.

As you read, consider the following questions:

1. According to corporations cited by the author, why should a CEO resign from his position for having an illicit marital affair?

2. How does Andrews define a "trait"?

3. What is an example of what the author suggests a job interviewer use to gauge a prospective employee's nature outside the office?

You probably have heard it from coworkers: "What I do on my own time has nothing to do with my job. I draw a line between my personal life and what I do at work."

If there is such a line between ethics on and off the job, though, it may be fainter than assumed. Consider, for example, Harry Stonecipher, who had to resign as CEO of Boeing [in 2005] after having an extramarital affair with a Boeing executive. Although the affair had not compromised Boeing's operational performance or financial condition, the company's chairman said in a prepared statement, "the facts reflected poorly on Harry's judgment and would impair his ability to lead the company."

Clearly, top-tier executives should take note of Stonecipher's spectacular fall. But what about the rest of us? Is there a relationship between personal ethics and business ethics, and, if so, what are its ramifications for hiring employees on every rung of the corporate ladder?

A number of ethicists and psychologists have begun challenging the cherished notion that we can keep our private selves and work selves separate. "We'd like to think there's a crisp line that divides the behaviors we do outside of work and those we engage in at work," says David Gebler, president of Working Values, a business ethics and training company in Sharon, Mass. But Gebler and others say the line is growing increasingly blurry.

More than an Abstract Issue

The relationship between private life and business life is not just an abstract philosophical issue. More companies, looking at recent high-profile corporate scandals, are searching for ways to avoid becoming the next front-page debacle. For HR [human resource] professionals, that creates pressure to take a candidate's ethics, both personal and business, into account when making decisions about hiring and promotion.

In a random survey of HR professionals conducted in May [2005] by the Society for Human Resource Management, more than four-fifths of 371 respondents either agreed or strongly agreed that organizations should take into account personal ethics and off-the-job behaviors when making hiring and pro-motion decisions. The online poll had a 5 percent margin of error.

"We certainly value family, religion and a hard-work ethic," says Denise Noel, director of quality and human resources at Dayton Freight Lines, a freight carrier in Dayton, Ohio. But she acknowledges that "what you do outside of work, we would probably never know. From the HR perspective, it would be very difficult to ascertain those things."

Yet there are clues—if you know where to look. . . . First, though, what about the fundamental questions: Are personal ethics and business ethics really two slides of the same coin? Or are we comparing pennies and nickels?

Bedrooms and Boardrooms

Most of us would like to believe there's at least some separa-tion between work and home. "My own view is that one's pri-vate life is private," says Dick Mason, a business professor and director of the Maguire Center for Ethics and Public Respon-sibility at Southern Methodist University in Dallas. "I think that ought to be the prima-facie viewpoint."

Mason, for one, doesn't believe that private lapses such as cheating on a spouse necessarily indicate a greater propensity for cheating, lying and stealing on the job. "I've certainly seen a lot of very successful and, I think, quite ethical executives who appeared to have an infidelity in their personal lives," says Mason. "As far as I was concerned, that was none of my business. And in those situations that I'm aware of, the personal infidelity hadn't flowed over to affect their business life."

However, "if you're going to cheat on your wife, who are you not going to cheat on?" asks Robert Hogan, former chair of the psychology department at the University of Tulsa and president of Hogan Assessment Systems, based in Tulsa, Okla., and Jacksonville, Fla. "Every guy I know who fools around is also a liar and a cheat in other ways. You just can't depend on them."

Hogan is the author of over 200 scholarly books, chapters and articles as well as developer of the Hogan Personality Inventory (HPI), a widely used, business-oriented personality test. He says the research data are clear on one point: "If you get work colleagues or subordinates to describe a person, and then you get the spouse and neighbors to describe the person, they all see the same individual."

When it comes to bad behavior, Hogan says there's an intrinsic link between embezzling, on one hand, and marital infidelity, public drunkenness, traffic tickets, fighting, vandalism and not paying one's personal bills, on the other. "All these things involve breaking the rules, and they're all motivated by hostility toward or disregard for authority."

The Science of Misbehavior

Indeed, a vast body of research shows that there are unifying themes in people's behavior—or misbehavior, as the case may be.

Psychologically speaking, a trait is a broad personality disposition that is relatively consistent across situations and generally stable over time. For the past 40 years, Marvin Zuckerman, a professor emeritus in the psychology department at

Ethics in the Workplace

The history of business in the United States is littered with tales of fraud, deceit and corruption, not only by the hands of a greedy few at the top, but also with the help of employees willing to go along with the charade.

Unethical behavior at the office can sometimes stem from a few "bad apples" among the bunch. . . .

But experts note that ethical breaches are often the result of the corporate culture or pressure from management, pressure that can emerge when a company finds itself unable to live up to financial forecasts or expectations and tries to bend the rules to achieve them, says Linda Treviño, professor of organizational behavior at Penn State's Smeal College of Business Administration.

"Most people will try to do what they're being asked to do because they want the company to succeed and they want to feel good about achieving their goals," says Treviño. "Most people do not have the moral development to resist those pressures." . . .

Catherine Valenti,
ABCNews.go.com, February 21, 2002.

the University of Delaware, has been studying something he calls the sensation-seeking trait. People who score high in this trait tend to act impulsively without thinking. They're driven to seek excitement and new experiences, and they're often willing to take risks in order to satisfy those needs.

Research has shown a strong association between behaviors such as substance abuse, sexual promiscuity and compulsive gambling. "It's the sensation-seeking trait that underlies many of these activities," says Zuckerman. Whether and how the trait is expressed at work depends on the situation. Zuckerman says that some sensation seekers choose jobs that offer enough variety to satisfy their need for change. Others bottle up their sensation-seeking tendencies at work, but let rip as soon as they get home. And still others who also have antisocial tendencies—in other words, an unwillingness or inability to conform to the accepted standards of society—get their kicks through criminal activities, including corporate crime. Explains Zuckerman, "Most high-sensation seekers are not antisocial, but almost all people with antisocial personalities are high-sensation seekers."

Taken to a pathological extreme, a lifelong pattern of misbehavior may be a sign of a condition known as antisocial personality disorder. Dr. Donald Black, a psychiatry professor at the University of Iowa College of Medicine and author of *Bad Boys, Bad Men: Confronting Antisocial Personality Disorder*, says between 2 percent and 3 percent of U.S. adults fall into this category. Some are in jail or on welfare, but others are sitting in boardrooms. As Black puts it in his book, "Antisocials are not just muggers, rapists and violent assailants. They sometimes are embezzlers, tax evaders, fraudulent businessmen, corrupt stock brokers and conniving attorneys."

Black has done research in which he looked up people decades after they were first diagnosed as being antisocial. "Most of them were still getting in trouble," says Black. "They remained severely impacted by their antisocial personality disorder even into their 70s and 80s." Black notes that their problems tended to extend across all spheres of life, including "their marriage, their finances and their work."

Insight Through Interviews

The bottom line: It would probably be very useful to know what a person is like both at work and at home before making a job offer, especially if it's a high-profile or sensitive position. The catch, as any HR professional knows, is that you're not allowed to ask job candidates many of the most obvious questions. The legal restrictions on what you can ask are intended to prevent discrimination and protect individual privacy. But they pose a challenge for HR professionals who want to gauge the fit between an individual's ethical standards and those of the company.

For example, even if your company defines personal ethics in terms of "family values," you still shouldn't ask prospective employees about their marital or parental status. And even if your employer defines personal morality in religious terms, you should still steer clear of any questions about a job candidate's religion.

"A lot of behavior that an academic or a philosopher might rely upon [in assessing a person's character] is just illegal to rely upon in a hiring situation." says Lester Rosen, president and CEO of Employment Screening Resources, a pre-employment screening firm in Novato, Calif.

What assessment options remain? One of the best is the integrity interview, says William Byham, who has a doctorate in industrial/organizational psychology and is chairman and CEO of Development Dimensions International, an HR training and consulting firm in Bridgeville, Pa. This type of employment interview is composed of carefully selected, open-ended questions. The interviewer first asks the job candidate about past ethical behavior, on the assumption that it's the best predictor of future conduct. The interviewer then asks probing follow-up questions to illuminate the thinking behind the reported behavior.

As a practical matter, Byham says, most integrity interviews include about three questions, which would add about 45 minutes to the standard interview process. Ideally, two or three people would conduct the interview. Byham recommends staying away from hypothetical questions, which lend themselves to facile, hypothetical answers. Instead, he advises asking about things people have actually done when faced with a work-related ethical dilemma.

For example: "Have you ever had to bend the rules or exaggerate a little bit when trying to make a sale?" Once the job candidate replies, the interviewer can probe with additional questions such as, "Can you give me another example?" Since the questions focus on work-related behavior, though, they give only an indirect indication of what the person might be like outside the office.

To get a better-rounded picture of the whole person, "we almost always try to engage someone at least once outside of the office setting," says Diane Malanowski, senior vice president of HR at SchoolNet, an educational software company in New York. Malanowski says you can pick up a multitude of clues about a person's character by simply having a restaurant meal together. "You'll see how they interact with the waiter or the people sitting at adjacent tables. I sometimes say, 'Gee, how much of a tip do you think we should leave?' Then, based on whatever percentage they suggest, I ask why. I want to see how they make those decisions. A lot of it bears on how they view the world in a more general sense."

| "Too many business schools do not take ethics training seriously. . . . As a result, the teaching of ethics, corporate social responsibility, and other business-and-society courses have been marginalized."

White-Collar Crime Is the Result of Business Schools Not Teaching Ethics

Kenneth R. Gray, Larry A. Frieder, and George W. Clark, Jr.

While many economists blame flaws in the capitalist system for the outbreaks of greed and crime, the three coauthors of the following viewpoint argue that corruption has been a part of most societies for thousands of years. They contend that virtue begins with the individual and that the first step in reduction of white-collar crime would be emphasizing the importance of ethics to business school students.

Kenneth R. Gray is professor of international management at the School of Business and Industry, Larry A. Frieder is professor

of financial services, and George W. Clark, Jr., is associate profes-
sor of organizational behavior and ethics, all at Florida A&M
University in Tallahassee.

As you read, consider the following questions:

1. What do the authors perceive as the benefits of a holistic approach to teaching business ethics?

2. Using a quote from newspaper columnist Leonard Pitts,
   how do Gray, Frieder, and Clark define the distinction
   between "reputation" and "character"?

3. Why do the authors claim it is beneficial to attach importance to the conduct of people in positions of power
   and authority?

In the long history of mankind, corruption was never considered extraordinary and neither were the proposals for
dealing with it. For example, the Indian political analyst,
Arthashastra Kautilya, in the fourth century B.C., artfully distinguished among forty different ways in which a public ser-
vant can be tempted or financially corrupted and described
how a system of spot checks followed by penalties and rewards could prevent these activities. He believed that a clear
system of rules and penalties, along with rigorous enforcement, could make a difference in behavior patterns.

Confucius believed the same result could be achieved by
clearly outlining the hierarchy of society, designating the
subordinate-superior axis in most relationships, and requiring
strict adherence to traditions of respect and obedience for all.
As [researchers Nansook] Park and [Christopher] Peterson explain,

> Confucius identified six relationships as crucial, those be-
> tween: ruler and subjects, parents and children, husband
> and wife, older brother and younger brother, teacher and
> student, and friend and friend. These relationships each
> have a "superior" and "subordinate" member, except for

friend and friend, although even here, if one individual is older than the other, it may become an older-younger brother relationship. In each relationship, the "subordinate" individual has the responsibility of obedience to the "superior," but only when the superior in turn displays benevolence and care.

A synopsis of the Confucian philosophy is presented by a pair of authors, [Calvin] Boardman and [Hideaki Kiyoshi] Kato, whose writings traced the historical connection between Confucian philosophical principles and the Japanese concept of kyosei. Although the philosophy of kyosei was initially developed during the sixteenth century in Japan, it was not until the twentieth century that the concepts were used to describe the business environment from an ethical viewpoint. The two Japanese characters of kyo (working together) and sei (life)

> suggest that corporations respect the interests of their stakeholders, including customers, staff, shareholders, suppliers, and competitors.... It is noteworthy that kyosei explicitly endorses a macro view of business ethics and corporate responsibility that encompasses the local and regional communities, the nation, the broader global community, in addition to the corporate community itself.

The Caux Round Table Report, was created by a group of Japanese, European, and U.S. business, education, and community leaders, and has as its foundation the ethical ideals of kyosei.

> These principles are rooted in two basic ethical ideals: kyosei and human dignity. The Japanese concept of kyosei means living and working together for the common good enabling cooperation and mutual prosperity to coexist with healthy and fair competition. Human dignity refers to the sacredness or value of each person as an end, not simply as a means to the fulfillment of others' purposes or even majority prescription.

The philosophical background of kyosei, lies squarely in "the way" of Confucius. The following is a sampling of what Confucius says.

- Reciprocity should be practiced throughout one's life. In short, one should treat others the way you would like to be treated.

- Virtue, not profit, should be the goal of the superior man.

- Life should be a balance between self-interest and altruism.

- One does not exist in isolation; we are a part of a larger and more complex family (literally and figuratively) where harmony can be achieved by acting appropriately with one another.

- Risk should be avoided by operating near the average, or the "golden mean," of possibilities.

- With respect to relationships, filial obedience to and respect for one's parents is paramount.

- One should love learning, live the simple life, practice what has been learned, and seek good teachers from whom one could continue learning throughout one's life.

The strength of Confucian philosophy contributed much to the concept of kyosei, and helped it to become a significant descriptor of corporate behavior in Japan and the rest of the world by the end of the twentieth century.

The dispersal and development of this cultural ideal, within all levels of society, helped to establish a virtuous process that became a cultural standard. The training of the young through family relationships most definitely helped to enshrine the Asian concept of filial piety that is still very prominent in Asian society today.

Peer Influence

Many societies rely on voluntary compliance with codes of behavior rather than on financial incentives to avoid corruption. A variety of behavioral norms, however, prevail in different societies. Plato suggested in *The Laws* that a strong sense of duty would help to prevent corruption, but he also noted that instilling this would be "no easy task." What is required is not just the general sense of dutifulness, but a particular attitude of compliance with rules, of strict conformity, which has a direct bearing on corruption. All of this comes under the general heading of what Adam Smith called "propriety." Rules of honest and upright behavior are not necessarily given priority in all codes of duty, but they certainly can provide a bulwark against corruption.

How people behave often depends on how they see—and perceive—others behaving. Much depends on the reading of prevailing behavioral norms. A sense of "relative propriety," a norm established by following the actions of a comparison group (in particular, others similarly placed) can be an important influence on behavior. Indeed, the argument that "others are doing the same" is one of the more commonly cited "reasons" for unethical behavior. The importance of imitation, and of following established "conventions," has been emphasized by commentators who felt moved to study the bearing of "moral sentiments" on social, political and economic life. Adam Smith noted:

> Many men behave very decently, and through the whole of their lives avoid any considerable degree of blame, who yet, perhaps, never felt the sentiment upon the propriety of which we found our approbation of their conduct, but *acted merely from a regard of what they saw were the established rules of behavior* (emphasis added).

In establishing "rules of behavior," importance may be particularly attached to the conduct of people in positions of power and authority. This makes the behavior of senior corporate officers especially important in setting norms of conduct. Indeed, writing in China in 122 B.C., the authors of Huinan Tzu stated the problem:

> If the measuring line is true, then the wood will be straight, not because one makes a special effort, but because that which it is *ruled* by makes it so. In the same way if the ruler is sincere and upright, then honest officials will serve in his government and scoundrels will go into hiding, but if the ruler is not upright, then evil men will have their way and loyal men will retire to seclusion.

Corrupt behavior in "high places" can have effects far beyond the direct consequences of that behavior, and the insistence on starting moral regulation at the top does have sound reasoning behind it. For example, the case of Adelphia is perhaps the most egregious instance of corporate self-dealing and financial chicanery in U.S corporate history. The infamous Rigas family, the founders of Adelphia, hid $2.3 billion in debts and treated the company as their personal "piggy bank," resulting in tens of billions of dollars in losses to investors. When the officers of a corporate body behave so, it is pointless to preach to the less powerful. . . .

Developing Character by Virtuous Behavior

Good character can be defined as a composite of qualities, typically of moral excellence and firmness blended with resolution, self-discipline, high principles, and sound judgment. Our character existed yesterday and will be with us tomorrow; character establishes both our day-to-day demeanor and our destiny. Can these virtues be instilled through education? If so, can they build character? Virtue is given as "a moral practice or action; conformity to a standard of right (divine law); moral excellence; integrity of character: uprightness of conduct."

Universal Symmetry: The Golden Rule Across Cultures

Culture	Teaching
Judaism	"Do not seek revenge or bear a grudge against one of your people: but love your neighbor as yourself." Bible, *Leviticus* 19:18 When he went to Hillel, he said to him," What is hateful to you, do not do to your neighbor: that is the whole Torah; all the rest of it is commentary; go and learn." *Talmud*, Shabbat 31a
Zoroastrianism	"That nature only is good when it shall not do unto another whatever is not good for its own self." *Dadistan*-I-Dink 94:5 "What is disagreeable to yourself do not do unto others." Shayast-na-Shayast 13:29
Buddhism	"Hurt not others in ways that you yourself would find hurtful." Udana-Varga 5:18
Confucianism	Tsetung asked, "Is there one word that can serve as a principle of conduct for life?" Confucius replied, "It is the word shu—reciprocity: Do not do to others what you do not want them to do to you." *Analects* 15.23 "Try your best to treat others as you would wish to be treated yourself and you will find that is the shortest way to benevolence." *Mencius* VII.A4
Jainism	"A man should wander about treating all creatures as hehimself would be treated." *Sutrakritanga* 1.11.33 "Therefore, neither does he [a sage] cause violence to others nor does he make others do so." *Acarangasutra* 5. 101-2

[CONTINUED]

Popular newspaper columnist Leonard Pitts writes that "reputation is about who you are when people are watching; character is about who you are when there is nobody in the room but you. Both matter, but of the two, character is far and away the most important. The former can induce others to think well of you, but only the latter allows you to think well of yourself." The ImClone scandal involving Martha Stewart is an example of how reputation and character are interre-

[CONTINUED]

Universal Symmetry: The Golden Rule Across Cultures

Culture	Teaching
Socrates	"Do not do to others what would anger you if done to you by others."
Hinduism	"One should not behave towards others in a way which is disagreeable to oneself. This is the essence of morality. All other activities are due to selfish desire." *Mahabharata*, Anusasana Parva 113.8
Hinduism and Brahmanism	"This is the sum of duty: Do naught unto others which would cause you pain if done to you." *Mahabharata* 5:15-17
Christianity	"Whatever you wish that men would do to you, do so to them." Bible, *Matthew* 7:12 "Do to others as you would have them do to you." Bible, Luke 6:31
Epictetus	"What you would avoid suffering yourself, seek not to impose on others."
Islam	"Not one of you is a believer until he loves for his brother-what he loves for himself." Forty Hadith of an-Nawawi 13
Baha'i	"And if thine eyes be turned towards justice, choose thou forthy neighbour that which thou choosest for thyself," *Epistleto the Son of the Wolf,* 30 "He should not wish for others what he does not wish for himself." Baha'u'llah

TAKEN FROM: Kenneth R. Gray, Larry A. Frieder, and George W. Clark, Jr., *Corporate Scandals: The Many Faces of Greed*, 2005.

lated. Martha Stewart built an empire atop beautiful living. Yet, her involvement with ImClone and her conviction for making false statements to federal agents cast suspicion on her character and tainted her reputation. The evidence of her unethical behavior and dubious character dragged down the reputation of her business.

Stephen R. Covey, the author of the best seller *The 7 Habits of Highly Effective People*, contends that:

> Character is made up of those principles and values that give your life direction, meaning and depth. These constitute your inner sense of what's right and wrong based not on laws or rules of conduct but on *who you are*. They include such traits as integrity, honesty, courage, fairness and generosity—which arise from the hard choices we have to make in life. . . . Many have come to believe that the only things we need for success are talent, energy and personality. But history has taught us that over the long haul, who we are is more important than who we appear to be.

Character can be developed through the practice of virtuous behavior. According to Aristotle, although we are endowed by nature with the capacity to acquire virtue, one is not naturally virtuous. One becomes virtuous by performing virtuous acts repeatedly until such acts become "second nature." At this point virtue is internalized, no longer a virtue of deed, but of character.

The Aristotelian assumption that virtuous behaviors (if practiced habitually) will help people develop into better human beings, would also support the assertion that good people can be good students, good business persons, good politicians and vice versa. The integration of virtue into the multiple roles that people play in their lives, at home and at work, will determine their ethical behaviors, and ultimately will define their character. . . .

Blindsided by Greed

During the early nineteen thirties, [economist] J.M. Keynes recognized that our modern economic practice was based on a moral inversion. He had written "of the pseudo-moral principles which have ridden us for two hundred years, by which we have exalted some of the most distasteful of human qualities into the position of highest virtue." Bald, disrespectful and single-minded aggressiveness that is understood to be destructive in other circumstances has become celebrated in corporate trenches as "competitiveness." Angry, egocentric lust for power that would qualify as tyranny in politics has been elevated to "strategic mastery" and "leadership" in business. And runaway greed has been sanctioned as "wealth creation," making heroes out of billionaire workaholics. The end seems to make the means irrelevant, so what is bad taste, bad judgment, or bad character in life has been made admirable and to be emulated in business.

Jane Eisner, a senior fellow at the University of Pennsylvania, explains how most Americans fail to acknowledge the degree to which greed has seeped into our national psyche and how it is skillfully justified by continued prosperity. Greed has become a sin masquerading as a reward and we seem to be absorbed by a false notion that wealth is a virtue. We have become "blinded by reality," or blinded to reality, and have come to believe that the wealthy must be virtuous. We no longer really recognize greed for what it is except in its most exaggerated displays.

USA Today reported in a major cover story how the former CEO of Tyco purchased a $15,000 umbrella stand and a $6,000 shower curtain. These are not virtuous acts. They are vicious ones, shameful products of the capital sin of avarice. Avarice (or greed) is "an insatiable desire to possess or acquire wealth or property far beyond what one needs or deserves; wanting or taking all one can get with no thought of the needs of others. . . ."

Eisner also argues that "built deep into the foundations of the advertising process [a major force behind our market driven economy] is the belief that we, as consumers, never have enough. Enough of what can vary with every 60-second commercial, but it's the sense of dissatisfaction, of yearning for some thing we didn't know we wanted that has turned citizens into consumers and 7-year-olds into the new target demographic." She adds, "who doesn't want more in a culture founded on manifest destiny, in an economy fueled by desire for the next new thing?"

So as a culture of consumers, what have we become? What is the result of this conditioning process that has caused us to believe in the pseudo-virtuous way of life? How has this way of living affected our relationships in our families, work groups, neighbors, and communities? Has this attitude of egotistic self-fulfillment affected our perceptions of right and wrong? If it has, is there hope of repairing this torn fabric in our society? Eisner sees the irony in the American psychological makeup that allows us to have strong religious beliefs while ignoring the fact that "every great religion in the world treats greed as the Mother of All Sins. Jesus, Muhammad, Buddha, the Tao Te Ching—all preached against the wanton desire of more than one requires or deserves." What are we to do? . . .

Education and Business Ethics

An alternative approach to educating future business leaders involves supplementing the traditional methods of teaching Business Ethics. Ethics are mainly taught on a purely cognitive level, with reading assignments, class lectures, group discussions of ethical dilemmas, and "case studies." This approach has been used for several decades in many business programs. Some of the content includes:

- studying business ethics issues, definitions, theories, and frameworks

- identifying and recognizing ethical issues

- understanding the interrelationship of ethics and social responsibility

- relating an ethical controversy in business to moral philosophy

- understanding the impact of significant others, of group influences, and of the corporate culture on an individual's decision making process

- choosing and defending a theory or principle that is used in resolving an ethical dispute or business decision

- examining the consequences of unethical and ethical business decisions

An alternative approach would include behavioral activities that attempt to help the individual student internalize the ethical information presented. Giving students the opportunity to practice good behaviors through various campus, community, industry, or volunteer service settings is one way that virtuous behavior could be internalized and reinforced, helping to cultivate character. Modules to address emotional change should also be considered. This might be accomplished through required "role playing" and/or transactional analysis. The goal would be to achieve both an affective and behavioral transformation in attitude patterns towards ethical behavior.

This suggested alternative for creating change involves an educational process that more comprehensively addresses the attitudes and moral character of graduates who will lead us in the future. As an alternative pedagogy, we would have a holistic approach to teaching business ethics. This holistic approach can be integrated into the Business Ethics course by teaching not only to the mind (cognitively), but also to the body (behavioral), as well as to the heart (affective).

Business programs have clearly proven the positive influence that their pedagogy can have on students. They, in general, graduate a very highly skilled group of individuals who join corporate America as leaders. The very power of their teaching suggests, however, that there is much more that can be done. The following suggestions surfaced at the 2003 meeting of the Academy of Management:

1. Too many business schools do not take ethics training seriously as part of their business curricula. Ethics courses are not perceived as serious or "core" courses, such as finance, accounting, and economics. As a result, the teaching of ethics, corporate social responsibility, and other business-and-society courses have been marginalized.

2. External organizations that do business school rankings, both nationally and regionally, could be of more assistance. Ethics courses and training should be a measured criterion that helps to determine these rankings. Currently, they are largely ignored and have no influence on the rankings.

3. The economic perspective dominates business school curricula. For all the good that economic perspectives do, they nonetheless emphasize a view of the world in dollars, profits, returns on investment, etc., which de-emphasizes other ways in which we might conceptualize the responsibilities and contributions of businesses to society.

In summary, the authors agree with these suggestions to effectively bring change to the business programs throughout the nation to assure the study of business ethics is taken as seriously as other academic core courses. It might be necessary to change the criteria of standards adopted by the accreditation agencies, i.e., the American Assembly of Collegiate Schools of Business, (AACSB) and include Business Ethics courses in the core of various curricula. In addition, the study of ethics should become part of the criteria used in the annual rankings of educational programs, which influences many individual decisions on where to study.

Overall, the importance of business ethics to any organization should be self-evident. It is just good business to have a reputation of ethical integrity among employees as well as customers and the general public. Instilling a greater sense of trust and honesty into our business culture will help to shape and support a corporate culture that will benefit all stakeholders: customers, employees, suppliers, and investors.

Sadly enough, as we have come to find out, when CEOs are bent on self-destruction, no amount of incentives to be good and no threatened punishments will stop their dysfunctional and/or illegal behavior. The cable operating company, Adelphia, is a case in point. The founding family that stood to gain the most from a successful and prosperous company, instead, chose to steal resources from the company coffers and consistently lied about it to their stockholders and board of directors. For change to be lasting, the laws of the land and the supervision by regulators must be buttressed by a healthy and ethical corporate culture. The culture must be buoyed by a set of values that are systematically established and constantly nurtured by corporate leaders, as well as by the society at large.

The Right Values

Despite the contributions of critical thinkers through the ages, most cultures and their associated institutions have had only limited success in achieving truly virtuous societies in which the behavior of individuals conformed with the culture's highest ideals. Various cultural codes have produced significant positive traits, but negative traits, sins, and other undesirable characteristics often appear. Given this time-tested reality, one must consider how a society such as the United States can promote virtuous behavior and simultaneously limit the presence of unavoidable negative traits such as greed, arrogance, dishonesty, and immorality.

Although the role of social institutions such as schools, religious groups, and family are relevant, our economic system puts a particular faith in the power of U.S. business schools to inculcate the "right" values and traits into its graduates, the individuals who will lead our economy in the future. Business schools' main course for addressing this important chore is Business Ethics. Unfortunately, this course has been found, for the most part, to be ineffective. For this reason we suggest several modifications and innovations to increase the efficacy of these courses.

In the larger context, it is ironic if not ridiculous that the general emphasis on ethics and much of the initial push for new ethics courses came from corporate executives in their role as advisors to business schools. . . . Large numbers of these same individuals were often found to be arrogant, greedy and insensitive to the broader community, if not actually engaged in some form of implicit and/or explicit corruption.

It would appear that business school professors could do a lot more, not only in their teaching but also in their consulting, public speaking, research and writing to speak out against these negative behaviors. Educators must clearly stand up against institutional failures such as those we have seen: the laxity of regulators at the SEC [Securities and Exchange Commission] and various self-regulating organizations such as the New York Stock Exchange and public accounting and auditing firms; the laxity and incompetence of responsible Boards of Directors or Boards of Trustees; and outrageous compensation packages for CEOs who performed poorly or were discharged.

When more difficult cases must be appraised or boundaries of acceptable behavior need to be established, academics can provide balanced perspective. Former General Electric CEO Jack Welch's retirement pay package appears deserving of this type of attention. Because he was undoubtedly one of the most effective and valuable corporate CEO's in U.S. history and played the lead role in enhancing GE's market value by tens of billions of dollars, few would question his receiving very large compensation. Nevertheless, when his divorce case resulted in the public disclosure of his huge retirement payments and seemingly endless perquisites, most Americans were aghast. Although Welch agreed to modify his package and lower his total compensation prospectively to quell criticism, it once again highlighted how complacently arrogant and greedy the U.S. management sector had become and that corporate directors remained complicit.

As a society, we must accept the fact that even if our cultural institutions, including business schools, work reasonably well, there will always be individual character defects and "fashionable," or broadly shared, negative traits that threaten to subvert the ethical code. For this reason, great attention must be given to the legal, regulatory, professional, and governance apparatus that oversees our free enterprise economic system to assure that our system continues to produce great wealth and concomitant standards of living.

> *"[White-collar criminals] want to be seen as brilliant businessmen with the Midas Touch, and will do anything it takes to maintain that impression and fund their lavish lifestyle."*

White-Collar Criminals Are Mentally Unbalanced People

Tom O'Connor

Although white-collar criminals require ingrained shrewdness, business acumen, and the capability to conceive and execute sophisticated planning, Tom O'Connor, the author of the following viewpoint, notes that mere possession of such skills does not make them psychologically sound personalities. According to O'Connor, most white-collar criminals are so accustomed to getting their way and living in such palatial luxury that it severely affects their ability to make rational judgments, let alone perceive their transgressions as illegal or unethical. In O'Connor's view, their wealth has turned business executives into sociopaths.

Tom O'Connor is a comparative criminologist whose articles have appeared in Contemporary Criminal Justice *and the* Encyclopedia of Criminology.

Tom O'Connor, "Intelligence Analysis of White Collar Crime," *MegaLinks in Criminal Justice*, January 21, 2006. Reproduced by permission.

As you read, consider the following questions:

1. According to the author, what are the three most common motives for property crime?

2. Why, in O'Connor's view, is it difficult to estimate the amount of foresight that goes on in the minds of white-collar criminals?

3. What are two of the reasons that the author speculates cause "pillars of the community" to become white-collar criminals?

The field of white collar crime in criminology has long been bogged down in conceptual and definitional debates. However, some things stay the same. It has been frequently remarked that the most common motives for property crime tend to fall into three categories which, in order of being the most frequent, are: (1) *to keep the party going* (money from the crime is used to purchase drugs); (2) *to keep up appearances* (money is used to buy expensive clothes, jewelry, or status items); and (3) *to keep things together* (money is used for living expenses, food, shelter, or child support).

[Criminologist Larry] Siegel defines white collar crime as *"illegal activities of people and institutions whose acknowledged purpose is profit through illegitimate business transactions."* To make it simple, white collar crime is larceny committed by a respectable, legitimate enterprise which is not set up to go out of business like an ordinary fraud or con game. White collar crime involves embezzlement, forgery, or fraud committed in the course of normal business practice, but is highly unethical and violates accepted accounting principles or the public trust. Like the crime of conspiracy, deception and cover up are the hallmarks of white collar crime. Sometimes the offender is a government official. Criminologists who work in this area sometimes approach white collar crime as the study of business crime, corporate crime, suite crime, crime at the top, elite crime, state crime, political crime, or governmental crime. Corporate espionage is sometimes included as a specialized area of study.

When [sociologist Edwin] Sutherland first coined the term white collar crime, and defined it as *"crime committed by a person of respectability and high social status in the course of his occupation,"* Sutherland basically was pointing out that poor people are not the only ones to commit crime. The color of the collar doesn't mean anything. It could be blue-collar or pink-collar crime. It is the generally accepted wisdom in criminology that although Sutherland's definition falls short in some ways, the underlying constructs of what he meant— deception and lack of physical force—remain constant, even while forms of the crime evolve. The NW3C [National White Collar Crime Center] definition is considered a good update: *"white collar crimes are defined as illegal or unethical acts that violate fiduciary responsibility or public trust for personal or organizational gain."* The [criminologist Herbert] Edelhertz typology includes: (1) crimes against government by public officials; (2) crimes against government by private citizens; (3) crimes against businesses; (4) crimes against investors; (5) crimes against consumers; (6) crimes against employees; and (7) crimes affecting public health. Something called the Green typology [of organization analyst Gary S. Green] includes: (1) crimes for the benefit of one's employer; (2) crimes by government officials; (2) crimes by professionals in the course of doing business; and (4) crimes by individuals in the course of their occupation.

There is *no uniform white collar crime reporting system.* The FBI only tracks crime data on embezzlement and fraud, so the best estimates are that 18,000 arrests for white collar crimes occur each year. The number of investigations far exceed that number, however. It appears prosecutions for crimes against consumers take priority over crimes against business and government. Offenders typically believe that whatever they've done is not wrong, and an expected entitlement or fringe benefit of their positions of power. Most research suggests that firms with declining profitability or budget cuts are more likely to break the law. Other research indicates that firms in highly regulated areas and volatile markets (like pharmaceuticals or petroleum) are more likely to break the law.

The Typical Profile

The typical white collar criminal is a white, middle class, educated male around 29 years of age (70% of the time) with no previous criminal history and no involvement in drug or alcohol abuse. Their offenses are characterized by sophisticated planning, and they have carefully considered lessons learned from the extensive histories most corporations have of regulatory violations. Most offenders prefer to work alone, except where the cooperation of others is needed. Almost all criminological theories (strain, learning, control, conflict, and neutralization) have been applied to white collar crime. The economic costs of white collar crime are staggering, running well into several billions a year. Perhaps more importantly, economic crime erodes public confidence.

The most common breeding ground, as [criminologist Diane] Vaughan points out, is the "free-wheeling, self-regulatory" work environment where the lines are blurred between acceptable and unacceptable business practices in the pursuit of profit. High levels of both internal and external competition as well as certain kinds of office politics will also create a breeding ground for white collar crime. As far as profiles go, the best research on the subject has been by [David] Weisburd et al., who studied 968 offenders over a 3 year period. It may be worth quoting from them, as follows:

> Most offenders are disproportionately white, middle-aged men who possess high levels of social capital, good income, and higher education (75% of the time). Most are married homeowners who occupy supervisory positions in their or-

ganizations. They do not usually have squeaky clean pasts, as about a third of the sample had at least one police arrest in their records, but they tended to stay away from violent crimes, and drifted in and out of property or public order crimes. Compared to ordinary criminals, white collar criminals begin and end their careers later, and include smaller numbers of recorded criminal events. However, they are similar to ordinary criminals in that they are unlikely to evidence a high degree of specialization and seem to age out of crime.

It is difficult to estimate the amount of planning or foresight that goes on in the minds of white collar criminals. This is so because most of them see their offending as simply an extension or exaggeration of normal operating procedures. For decades, criminologists have maintained that neutralizations play an important role in the initial stages of planning a white collar crime. Neutralizations are like rationalizations, except they are the kinds of things one says to himself before (not after) the crime is committed. Some offenders, like the ones [criminologist Amber] Horning describes, engage in a sort of "cognitive mapping" where certain property and certain procedures in the organization are perceived as "fair game" for criminal activity. Other, so-called "rogue" employees sometimes claim they were just following implicit orders. Cressey (1953) used the phrase "vocabularies of adjustment" to describe the many ways in which white collar criminals comfort or deny their guilty minds, and it has become conventional in criminology (since Cressey) to talk about whether such criminals had an unshareable "problem" or perceived some "threat." The "problem" school of thought holds that something like the 3 B's (babes, booze, and bets)—a problem with infidelity, alcohol or drugs, or a gambling or debt problem—is at root of the criminality. The "threat" school of thought holds that something in the competitive environment of the organization or in the potential offender's career path is at the root of the problem. One will find criminologists about equally divided over this issue.

One of the more prominent theories is that offenders possess an "unshareable financial problem", the result of living beyond their means, piling up gambling debts, etc. (the three Bs: Babes, Booze, Bets), and feel they cannot let anyone know about their situation without ruining their reputation. Other theories stress the "culture at the top" notion, which sets the tone for the ethical climate in the organization. The whole world of business is kept in line by what is called "economism"—a self-regulating compliance strategy based on the deterrent effects of economic sanctions and civil penalties. This inherently places a lot of trust in the personalities of those who work in business.

Regardless of the motivation, the offenders are probably as complex as the laws and regulations in this area. The required mental states, for example, range from "negligently" to "recklessly" to "knowingly", depending upon what type of white collar crime you're talking about. Prosecution, or more specifically, deciding who prosecutes, opens up a cornucopia of agencies, all with joint and/or overlapping responsibilities. In some cases, the level of cooperation is well-known, such as between the FBI (threat of criminal charges) and FTC [Federal Trade Commission] (civil cease & desist orders), but OSHA [Occupational Health and Safety Administration] inspectors have only recently been equipped with police powers, and the investigative arms of many other agencies are not well known. . . .

Lifestyle Factors and Indicators

CEOs don't travel First Class, they travel *Their Class* in private jets—no lines, no mingling with the peons, and their favorite toy (business expense) is the Gulfstream G450 jet, which flies 5,000 miles nonstop, costs $33 million, and is equipped with deerskin seats, mahogany cabinets, Persian carpets, flat-screen

Is Public Shaming a More Effective Deterrent than Prison Time?

The population of top corporate executives in America can be characterized as living in an exclusive small town. As Edward Rock has pointed out, "the senior managers and directors of large, publicly held corporations, and the lawyers who advise them—form a surprisingly small and close-knit community. The directors of large, publicly held corporations number roughly four to five thousand." In such a community, information travels, impressions are formed and hardened, loyalties are tested, and reputations are built and dismantled, extremely efficiently, often with just a few phone calls. In a rarefied community such as this, the role of reputation is significant. CEOs after all, and the directors with whom they work, are status-conscious creatures. The reason many of them seek high corporate office or serve on corporate boards in the first place often has to do with visibility and personal prestige.

Successful executives typically conduct themselves so as to enhance the perception that they are wise and all-knowing, that their judgment is valued by others, and that they move in influential public circles. They serve on charitable boards, for example, and participate as distinguished speakers at university functions. Some participate in politics; others write autobiographies. Many subject themselves willingly to the hagiography of the business press. Challenges to these men's and women's reputations consequently are not taken lightly—and events that cast them or their business skills in an unflattering light may have a particularly dramatic impact upon them. . . .

Jayne W. Barnard,
Southern California Law Review, *vol. 72, no. 4, 1999.*

video displays with surround-sound systems, walk-in showers, and 24K gold plated fixtures. Arrogance, rudeness, and imperiousness characterize their relationships with others, and their lifestyles can be described as nothing other than opulent and lavish. Once the adored "white knights" of the US economy, CEOs and their glamorous lifestyles began to fall from grace with the stock market crash in 2001 and the Enron scandal in 2002. Juries are finding it easier and easier to return findings of guilt or fault because they simply cannot identify with the level of selfish greed involved. What is it, however, that turns a "pillar of the community" into a corporate criminal? There are several speculations, none of which are really well-supported by criminological research, but interesting nonetheless.

#1: They think they can get away with it—usually one part of the corporation is doing quite well, and profits are climbing astronomically. The profits from this "sector" are siphoned off for personal use, but some of it is funneled back to keep the rest of the corporation from deteriorating. It's usually only when one part of the corporation is experiencing huge losses that attention is attracted.

#2: Pure greed, delusions of grandeur, or megalomania—usually the executive is mixing in high-class company and wants to impress such folks as having the trappings of power. They want to be seen as brilliant businessmen with the Midas Touch, and will do anything it takes to maintain that impression and fund their lavish lifestyle.

#3: Psychopathic tendencies—usually they have bullied their way to the top, learned to "top off" their salary by raiding the corporate coffers, and developed a coterie of followers and yes-people who constantly tell them how great they are. A large portion of these offenders are discovered after a failed office romance or sexual escapade.

#4: Creative opportunities and corruption—usually the executive is put in charge of an overseas operation and because

they want to see those operations succeed, succumb to the bribery and corruption prevalent in many foreign nations, and get caught up in a slippery slope of moral decline where they end up robbing from their own corporation.

There are obviously more speculations that could be made, and one would be hard pressed to explain things like the finding that CEOs usually cheat at golf, but it's clear that an appetite for risk-taking is prevalent among senior business executives. There are only somewhere between 4,000 and 5,000 top CEOs that are part of America's "leadership class," and this is a tight, close-knit community, driven by reputation and status-consciousness. For this reason, many criminologists have said that something like "reintegrative shaming" or "woodshedding" might work at deterring them from criminal conduct. Woodshedding is a unique legal term in corporate law which takes advantage of the so-called "corporate icon" clause in (somewhat rare) cases where the corporation as a whole has been found guilty or pled guilty to a crime, but criminologists have been calling for its expanded use. Top executives are frequently so status-conscious that if a judge is willing to consider an alternative sentence like a "shaming ritual," the theory is that it will have more of an effect than some fine or sanction imposed by an impersonal, remote legal authority.

> *"[White-collar] offenders consider the risk posed by their individual role, the personal consequences, and the consequences for the organization. . . . These complexities are indicators of the rationality of organizational crimes."*

White-Collar Criminals Are Rational Persons

Neal Shover and Andy Hochstetler

Although criminals are by definition social deviants, corporate crimes tend to be well-planned organizational activities committed with the implicit approval and support often of many fellow employees. In the following viewpoint, authors Neal Shover and Andy Hochstetler claim studies show that in the modern business world, illegal acts are widely encouraged as a sign of good "team-playing" and those who do not "play ball" soon find themselves without a job. According to reliable statistics, the authors note, most perpetrators are fully aware of the penalties for being caught but feel certain that they will not be apprehended and that either way the potential payoff far outweighs the risk.

Neal Shover is a professor of sociology at the University of Tennessee, Knoxville and the author of Great Pretenders: Pur-

Neal Shover and Andy Hochstetler, from *Choosing White Collar Crime*. Cambridge University Press, 2006. Reproduced by permission.

suits and Careers of Persistent Thieves. *Andy Hochstetler is an associate professor of sociology at Iowa State University and the author of numerous articles on criminology.*

As you read, consider the following questions:

1. What are two examples described by the authors of sources of crisis that a white-collar criminal might view as "threats to shares-seeking or status-maintaining behavior"?
2. According to Shover and Hochstetler, what makes white-collar crime unique by occurring in organizational and industrial environments?
3. What is one of the parallels the authors draw between white-collar crime and street crime?

For nearly three decades investigators have explored how street criminals estimate the costs and benefits of crime and how they make criminal decisions. A great deal is known about their daily rounds, the contexts wherein they make criminal decisions and the dynamics of the process. A variety of methodologies have been used to examine these matters, but ethnographic studies unquestionably have shed the most revealing light. Most, for example, show that thieves are rational when it comes to choosing targets that offer security and the surest returns.

In broad outline, investigators have demonstrated that street offenders generally behave consistent with predictions based on rational-choice theory. They commit crime with an eye toward maximizing reward and minimizing risk. Research makes clear, however, that burglars, armed robbers, and other street criminals are anything but careful calculating actors. This body of research serves as a useful starting point for anyone interested in white-collar criminal decision making whether the results are cast as accident, scandal, or mistake.

Much to Gain, Little to Lose

A high proportion of street offenders break the law in the context of lifestyles that make it seem there is much to gain and little to lose by doing so. Skid-row addicts facing withdrawal may see great utility in $100 while the shame of stealing or getting caught seems negligible. Street offenders usually have little more than a hunch about their chances of apprehension, and in moments of clarity, many understand that arrest probably awaits if they continue in crime. In less reflective moments, like those that precede most crimes, they conclude that they probably can get away with at least one more offense. Their decisions generally take only an instant and result from hasty, rudimentary, and imprecise calculation. Interviews with 113 men convicted of robbery or an offense related to robbery revealed, for example, that "over half . . . reported no planning at all". The criminal ambitions of most are limited to fulfilling an immediate desire.

One reason for spontaneity is that street offenders' decisions are made in the context and dynamics of street life and hustling. As the context of decision making, hustling helps explain why research on 105 active residential burglars found that they expressed a "steadfast refusal to dwell on the possibility of being apprehended". Street offenders develop an ability to put out of mind risk to self and others, to focus on the potential payoffs of specific criminal acts and steel themselves to go ahead. Those who hustle continuously develop an alert opportunism that prepares them to see opportunity where others do not. They can react instantly and with little thought when they encounter something promising.

A substantial majority of street crimes occur in groups, and interpersonal dynamics constrain decision making. Conversation and interactional dynamics build confidence and excitement by emphasizing positive outcomes and the ability of those present to accomplish the task while downplaying the risks. Offenders call these exchanges "talking it up" or "pump-

119

ing each other up". Both the substance and tone of these discussions are influenced by drugs and alcohol or the immediate need for more.

Drug use and altered states of consciousness inevitably result in crude and hasty calculation. Youth and mood also and can make salient preferences and commitments that relegate caution to the background. Danger and excitement that are attributes of street crime repel most but attract some. Young and intoxicated offenders looking for opportunity to prove their mettle often misjudge the potential for considerable cost and meager benefit. The circumstances in which street offenders live and play complicates immensely the challenge of frightening them into compliance.

White-Collar Criminal Choice

Much less is known about white-collar offender decision making; there are far fewer offender autobiographies and ethnographic studies to draw from. Interviews of ordinary embezzlers and fraudsters show that the appeal of these crimes is rooted in troublesome situations at work or in other areas of life that lead the offender to be alert to opportunities. Embezzlers strongly prefer solutions that allow them to keep financial problems secret and that do not erode reputations or undermine ascribed obligations. Criminal opportunity is attractive as a means of responding to desire to assist family crises or forestalling a fall. There are many sources of crisis, but previous business reversed, trouble with employers, family difficulties, or vices and other personal shortcomings are typical. All come to represent for the individual "threats to status-seeking or status-maintaining behavior" (Cressey). When combined with changes in social environment the odds of crime are increased. Individuals who suffer business reversals can become socially isolated with nowhere to turn for solutions to their financial problems. Multiple conditions contribute but preference is the same for many ordinary offenders, a financial solution that postpones revelation of secretive problems or postpones painful consequence. Women who are unattached to the workforce do it to satisfy their habits or to support domineering men. They are more likely to commit fraud than embezzlement because that is the best opportunity they have. Those that are attached to the workforce are likely to be attempting to enhance family finances by crime and are likely to embezzle. All make the best of the criminal opportunities that they have. The pressures of relatively conventional home lives and lives of unemployment can inspire desire for instantaneous payoff. . . .

For most ordinary white-collar offenders, objective circumstances have changed little directly before their offense, but their receptiveness to the draw of lure increases as problems become pressing or turmoil distract them. Confronted with mounting pressures and disruptions, compliance seems to require too much effort and individuals reach what they experience as a breaking point. They mentally let go of or loosen the commitments that previously restrained them. Those who can reconcile violating financial trust with a positive self-concept are at increased risk to commit crime. Upperworld and organizational criminal decision making is shrouded in fog, but it is likely that the problems that lead upperworld offenders to crime are less personal and pressing. . . .

Crime and Context

The way offenders become aware of and weigh opportunity varies by history and circumstance. Evidence is amassing that some preferences and outlooks that increase the appeal of crime, for example, form early in life. With differing abilities to calculate accurately and varied ends in mind, offenders consider the costs and rewards of offending versus the repercussions of deciding not to for their own lives and in context. Individual and contextual variation constrain how options are assessed and decisions are made in both background and foreground. Choices, moreover, occur in sequences and change as circumstances develop. Moral reservations and internal inhibitions are subject to situational suspension or inattention. The lenses through which offenders see criminal opportunity and make decisions are colored by the social contexts where crime occurs.

The context for many criminal decisions are those in which white-collar labor. Many white-collar workers devote more time and thought to work and career than to anything else and they are sensitive to cues and messages they receive at work. Their criminal decisions, especially in the upper ranks, are likely to be complex and to take into account many variables and circumstances. The structure and history of the industries where employees operate are important contextual determinants. Organizational actors often have a keen grasp of market and organizational forces that constrain their behavior. Their preferences, commitments, and utilities are adjusted to suit their industrial and organizational location and what is demanded of them. A risk-averse decision maker would not remain employed at the trading desks of some stock firms long. A salesman in an industry where bid-rigging is prevalent may take some time to discover from peers and superiors that price stability and predictability in the industry override benefits of the firm's short-term returns. Once the advantages are understood bid-rigging might result. Internal compliance specialists can be taught the promotion depends on identifying misconduct and finding ways to hide it from outsiders. Salespersons get the message when their quotas go up despite regular memos from company lawyers that the practices that led to previous sales are on unsteady legal ground. Long-term employment in an industry or organization can familiarize employees with potential criminal solutions to problems the inexperienced will only discover with time. In some industries, illegal opportunities and how to exploit them guiltlessly is part of the collective ethos. . . .

Organizational Justifications

Organizational influences often are exerted and experienced in subunits of an organization. Dictates and demands from above are assumed to be authoritative in organizations, but people look to those around them for help in interpreting signals and deciding what to do in daily decisions. The line between what the organization demands and what workmates expect often is difficult to draw. Mature adults will walk away from friends that are pushing them in undesirable directions when they are not at work; it may not be as easy where livelihoods are on the line. Regular and structured meetings make gradual adjustments to moral codes and prodding resistant offenders more likely than it is in casual relationships. Regular contact and formal ties between white-collar co-offenders build allegiance, particularly when a secret is shared that places everyone at risk.

Criminal decisions in organizations sometimes are the result of careful and routine problem solving. People are sent home with problems and decisions to ponder and they reassemble at regularly scheduled intervals to assess developments and adjust strategies. Decision making occurs in many minds incrementally, over time, and only eventually by consensus. Not all organizational crimes are so, but in some there is a complex division of labor and a formal procedure for reaching a decision. Criminal ideas may be passed between relevant players and across organizational subunits. Participants may bounce them off workmates, submit them to superiors or bring them to a vote. In a high-profile corporate price-fixing conspiracy of the 1990s, conspirators believed and decided that rigging markets was to their corporate advantage. The decision was not made, however, until agreement could be reached and details arranged. The meetings resembled those for licit but secretive deals. Early conversations were held in private rooms over drinks. Participants were vague and cautious. They avoided words like "agreement" that were too precise and that could be used against them in court. Other meetings that were thought to be safe because all were insiders and surveillance was highly unlikely were casual. In many, the purpose was overt. Visual aids sometimes were used to help arrange prices. Participants in the illegal projects were informed of progress in negotiating terms of agreements at each stage, but they concerted ignorance and maintained plausible deniability where convenient. Complex and carefully managed decision making is part of the white-collar world. A Wall Street trader recalls that his idea was sparked by escalating investment losses. Despite the urgency, a plan was developed by considering past actions, presenting solutions and ideas to peers, and then checking with superiors to make sure the decision was feasible and approved. . . .

When a web of conspirators has a mutual understanding of how everything should work, the trepidation and uncertainty characteristic of many crimes is avoided. Decision making is routinized, divided, and designed both to hide criminal intent and to ensure that uninformed or scrupulous outsiders do not throw a cog in the wheels. No party need discuss or admit what is going on explicitly; business can be conducted smoothly and as if it was legitimate.

Much of the distinctiveness of white-collar crime derives from the fact that it often occurs in organizational and industrial environments. Multiple people, subunits and tasks contribute to goals, perceptions and values at work and these influences shift constantly as new situations arise. Performance pressure and criminogenic cultural conditions coupled with bureaucratic and hierarchical arrangements shape motivations, preferences, and decision-making dynamics. Offenders consider the risk posed by their individual role, the personal consequences, and the consequences for the organization. Standing arrangements and support sometimes ease the crimes. These complexities are indicators of the ratio-

Characteristics of Individuals Sentenced for Federal Street Crimes and White-Collar Crimes, United States, 1995–2002

Characteristic	Street offenders[a]	White-collar offenders[b]
Race (percent African American and Hispanic)	48.5	32.3
Gender (percent male)	92.8	72.7
Education		
Less than high school	38.6	17.1
High school graduate	39.7	28.7
Some college	18.4	30.2
College graduate	2.8	19.5
Age		
Under 21	10.4	1.6
21–30	41.8	24.6
31–40	29.1	29.4
41–50	15.7	25.0
50+	7.2	20.5
Average age	31.8	44.2
Average number of cases annually	2,600	8,205

[a]Includes defendants convicted of murder, manslaughter, assault, robbery, burglary, and auto theft.
[b]Includes defendants convicted of fraud, embezzlement, bribery, tax offenses, antitrust offenses, and food and drug violations.
Source: U.S. Sentencing Commission. Sourcebook of Federal Sentencing Statistics. (1997–2001).

TAKEN FROM: Neal Shover and Andy Huchstetler, *Choosing White-Collar Crime*. Cambridge University Press, pg. 53, 2006.

nality of organizational crimes. Organizations are predictable environments where logic and planning pay.

Doing Deals

Deals are business transactions with negotiable terms. Deals are cultivated through social contacts and financial investments. "The social factors that bind managers to one another, whether in conflict or harmony, are the chief source of deals," [according to sociologist Robert Jackall]. The way deals typically are done in an organization and the industry where it is located are significant determinants of organizational structure and norms. Likewise, the formal arrangement of deals can make the decision to commit crime seem small. For example, the privileged information gained by key positions in institutional networks and constant jockeying for position among corporate brokers makes them attentive to opportunities found in insider trades. The structure of deals in an industry or organization play a significant part in the distribution of criminal opportunity.

The process of deal making and communication during it also has characteristics that potentially make criminal opportunity attractive. An important part of committing crime is the process of "anaesthetizing the conscience" with rhetorical and linguistic devices, and these devices may be shared among members of an organization or profession. Conversations that precede crime often contain excuses, frustrations, reasons why crime should be done or indications that it is normal procedure. Deals are promising settings for talk that obscures moral components of decisions and that insulates participants from consideration of adverse consequences. They are competitive.

Deals have a contrived, artificial quality that allows participants to suspend reservations against aggressively seeking advantages that affect transactions in other spheres. Deal making is viewed by insiders as a game in which players manipulate others to desired ends. Game metaphors capture the maneuvers and manipulations found in many deals without raising unpleasant and morally unsettling connotations. Interests that are at odds characterize the most mutually beneficial business arrangements. Those who enter a deal have consented to complete, and recognizing this allows competitors to be manipulative or deceptive while maintaining a favorable view of themselves. The ethical barriers against crime are thinned in the process of deal making. In some business cultures and transactions, prevarications are common and viewed as expressions of optimism and salesmanship.

Interaction between insiders is as important for understanding deals as interaction with outside partners or victims. It is well known that presentation of alternatives as well as their substance affects decisions. Presentation is a substantial part of the artfulness of deals. In attending to the positives and glossing over problems, inertia builds and qualms recede, Criminal statutes can be framed as negotiable technicalities or unrealistic ideals, rather than as inflexible standards that prevent harm. Reasons that crime is necessary in an industry or organization can be recited in a timely manner to make sure that potential participants are in agreement and to convince the reluctant. Reservations can be argued and countered. The result is that the law's ability to influence a decision is diminished. A *Wall Street Journal* reporter who wrote stories and provided them in advance to a high-placed trader so that they could profit illegally recalls the interaction that obscured his ethical and professional obligations:

> I respected the *Journal* and my profession . . . and would not have agreed to any arrangement that required me to misinform in any way the editors or readers of my columns.
>
> 'Oh yeah!' he said enthusiastically. 'That's right. You just keep doing what you're doing. The only difference is you tell me what the column's about. I won't bother you about your business and you won't bother me about mine.'
>
> Another thing is I probably would be better off not knowing how much money you're making. I know that sound's funny but in a way I think it might make my job harder if I knew we'd make a ton of money. . . .'
>
> 'You write the columns and I'll make the trades. No one gets hurt, no one knows. Then, when we've got a few million bucks stashed away, I'll start my own firm and you'll come work for me. Deal?' [quoted from R. Foster Winans, *Trading Secrets*].

As different as the context is from that of the street offender, this description shows that white-collar offenders also [according to criminologist Diane Vaughan,] "talk it up" in their approach to crime. . . .

Threat and Choice

Both street criminals and white-collar criminals calculate before committing crime; both choose to break the law. Investigators of white-collar crime generally have ignored research on decision making by other types of offenders and the similarities to decision making by white-collar offenders. Evidence is not compelling or voluminous, but it suggests, for example, that street offenders and white-collar offenders weigh the potential payoffs from crime more heavily than the estimated risks. They focus on immediate reward and shortcuts to goals and may fail to see moral implications that affect others. Individual propensity shapes what they weigh and choose. Many operate in environments where they "carry on as if nothing were wrong when they continually face evidence that something [is] wrong.". In the presence of like-minded companions, they can put out of mind how the larger public would judge their action and thereby blunt the deterrent effect of legal threats. In their efforts to cope with immediate crisis and daily hassles, these become remote and ill-considered contingencies. Rational-choice theory accommodates this contextual and individual variation. [Criminologist David] Weisburd and associates remark that:

> one implication of our emphasis on crisis and opportunity is that crimes committed by people in our sample often involve decision-making processes that are, within their context and in the understanding of the offender, reasoned. In this sense, the offenders we study appear to follow a rational model of offending.

While-collar crime is committed because some people estimate the payoff as greater than the risks or consequences of being caught. Seen in this way, it is sound crime-control policy to escalate the perceived risks of it while increasing legitimate opportunities and perceived payoff from noncriminal conduct. The key lies in using public policy to constrain individual decision making so that those who consider crime do not find it to be a profitable option. . . .

Research on target hardening and situational crime prevention shows that few street offenders will choose to offend when the odds of being caught near certainty, where success requires creativity or significant effort, and where returns will be insignificant. Accounting firms that inflate earnings estimates to meet quarterly objectives, grocery clerks who ring employee discounts for friends, and street-corner drug dealers share a potential for significant painful consequences and are alike in this: many either ignore or view as unlikely these contingencies. Few clear-headed offenders with anything appreciable to lose would commit crime if they thought criminal prosecution or long-term imprisonment were likely consequences. Most are aware that their acts have the potential for criminal penalties if things go badly, but that is not the outcome they expect. They hope to avoid penalties by hiding their intent and responsibility. Like street offenders, most white-collar offenders do not pin their hopes on the number of months prescribed by the sentencing tables for convicted felons but on avoiding entirely this penalty.

> *"However they're punished, white-collar criminals are clearly different from other criminals because they usually have good salaries and hefty bank balances."*

White-Collar Criminals Tend to Be Wealthy

Cynthia Crossen

Although detractors claim that people of modest income levels can technically commit what legally qualifies as white-collar crime, Cynthia Crossen, the author of the following viewpoint, argues that the very phrase "white-collar" refers to crimes committed specifically by the affluent. Crossen also cites studies conducted by scholar Edwin Sutherland, who first coined the phrase in 1939 and defined it as illegal activities committed by people of "respectability and high social status." Crossen also notes that corporate crimes existed for decades in America before being formally recognized as violations of the law.

Cynthia Crossen is a columnist and former senior editor of the Wall Street Journal. *Her books include* The Tainted Truth *and* The Rich and How They Got That Way.

As you read, consider the following questions:

1. According to the author, until the twentieth century, what was the prevailing ethic for people who bilked the public?

2. What is Crossen's definition of "diffuse victimization"?

3. What are two theories mentioned by the author that experts in different fields have given about what might cause rich people to steal?

Before [sociologist] Edwin Sutherland, most criminologists believed that theft was a pathological reaction to poverty.

But in 1939, Mr. Sutherland, a widely respected sociology professor at Indiana University, coined a new term: white-collar crime.

People of "respectability and high social status," Mr. Sutherland asserted, broke laws as often as members of the lower classes, but the government, media and public didn't think of them as criminals. Until scholars accepted that affluent and reputable people also steal, Mr. Sutherland argued, they would never truly understand the criminal mind.

Sutherland had begun his study of the "criminals of the upper world" by counting the adverse legal decisions against 70 of America's largest corporations since their founding.

Not a single one had an unblemished record. Two—Armour & Co. and Swift & Co.—had 50 violations each for offenses such as financial fraud, restraint of trade and false advertising. The average was 14.

The pervasiveness of law breaking in corporate America convinced Mr. Sutherland that the conventional wisdom about economic crime was wrong. If poverty was the primary risk factor, why were so many successful professionals doing it? Furthermore, he discarded the notion that white-collar criminals were "rotten apples," individuals born with a predisposition to steal. White-collar crime is learned behavior, Mr. Sutherland argued, a consequence of corporate cultures where regulation is regarded as harassment, and profit is the measure of the man.

Quoting the 19th-century white-collar scoundrel Daniel Drew, Mr. Sutherland writes: "A prickly conscience would be like a white silk apron for a blacksmith. Sometimes you've got to get your hands dirty, but that doesn't mean the money you make is also dirty. Black hens can lay white eggs."

Until the 20th century, a person who bilked the public without using force was rarely prosecuted. Caveat emptor—buyer beware—was the prevailing ethic. Or as one early-20th-century judge said, "We are not to indict one man for making a fool of another." The so-called robber barons of the 19th century, such as Daniel Drew, who literally invented the term "watered stock," didn't even get a slap on the wrist.

Regulating Profit

Then came the Sherman Antitrust Act (1890), the Federal Trade Commission (1914), the Securities and Exchange Commission (1934), and a host of other laws and regulations that attempted to set limits on what people can do in the name of profit. Yet, while white-collar infractions were deemed illegal, they still weren't necessarily criminal.

"Most of the defendants in antitrust cases aren't criminals in the usual sense," wrote Wendell Berge, an assistant U.S. attorney general, in 1940. "There is no reason why antitrust enforcement requires branding them as such."

It wasn't until 1961 that any business executives convicted of violating the Sherman Act actually went to prison.

In the decades since Mr. Sutherland classified white-collar crime, criminologists have argued fervently about his work. Some believe that only cases adjudicated by criminal courts are crimes. Others say there's an obvious difference between staring down a gun barrel and losing some retirement savings. White-collar crime has "diffuse victimization," as it's described:

Upper- vs. Lower-Class Crimes

The upper class commits far more crime than the lower class. Street criminals stole $15.3 billion in 1993, but white collar-criminals embezzled $200 billion. Street criminals murdered 23,271 people that year, but the decisions of profit-driven corporations murdered at least 318,368 (through pollution, consumer and worker safety violations, etc.) Corporations deserve blame for these deaths because they lobby for and enact policies which drive up these death rates. Virtually all other rich countries have higher safeguards and lower death rates.

Steve Kangas, www.luppin.com, 2004.

There are usually many victims over a long period of time. The thief and victim almost never come face to face. The crimes are complex and difficult even for other business executives to understand.

That helps explain why, in a single day recounted by Christopher Stone in his 1975 book, "Where the Law Ends," two cases being decided in a Georgia court ended so differently. In one case, an embezzler had stolen $4.6 million from a bank. In the other, three men had robbed a bank of about $14,000. The embezzler was sentenced to 10 years in jail; the robbers received 16 years each.

However they're punished, white-collar criminals are clearly different from other criminals because they usually have good salaries and hefty bank balances. The question of why a rich person steals has also been the subject of lively debate. One psychiatrist theorizes that such people have a "fantasy of omnipotence," and are guided by the "common business ideal of success at any price." Another sociologist has suggested that because many business people are ambitious, competitive and aggressive, they experience a feeling of tension that must be relieved somehow, sometimes by stealing.

Still another posits that business people face contradictory expectations: As a citizen, they're supposed to obey the law, but as an executive, they're supposed to resist the law whenever possible. C. Wright Mills blamed white-collar crime on "structured immorality," an impersonal corporate culture and a lack of personal responsibility among executives.

Mr. Sutherland never pinpointed the reason why some business executives steal, and others don't. But he did lament the costs of such crimes, and not just the economic ones. "White-collar crimes," he wrote, "violate trust and thus create distrust, and this lowers social morale and produces social disorganization on a large scale."

> "Most of the scandals that have beset Corporate America have deep roots in dysfunctional organizations, the dictates of which too frequently overwhelm an employee's better angels."

White-Collar Criminals Tend to Be Victims of Corporate Culture

Paul Sweeney

While the most popular conception of the white-collar criminal is that of the rich CEO, Paul Sweeney, the author of the following viewpoint, argues that most corporate crimes require the compliance of numerous underlings. Many businesspeople, Sweeney claims, are fundamentally honest individuals who, as a result of the brutally competitive nature of the modern business culture, find themselves compelled to cover up the illegal, unethical actions of their superiors, and risk consequent prison time, simply in order to avoid losing their jobs.

Paul Sweeney is a business writer in Brooklyn, New York.

Paul Sweeney, "Fraud: What Starts Small Can Snowball," *Financial Executive*, vol. 19, December 2003, pp. 18–20. Copyright © 2003 Financial Executives Institute. Reproduced by permission.

As you read, consider the following questions:

1. According to the author, what do experts in the field of law cite as a crucial lesson to be learned from high-profile corporate fraud cases of the last decade?

2. In Sweeney's view, what are the two common characteristics of the "corporate swamps" that serve as a breeding-ground for fraud?

3. What are two examples the author mentions as newly enacted control methods designed to help put an end to white-collar crime?

The situation is vexing. You are a mid-level financial manager at a company, and you're attending a meeting with Wall Street analysts. Your boss—who just happens to be the company's chief financial officer [CFO]—brilliantly reels off an array of statistics projecting a rosy picture of growth in revenues and net earnings. Too bad that the numbers are inflated and untrue.

Suddenly and without warning, the CFO looks over at you and demands corroboration. "Isn't that correct?" he demands.

Welcome to the hot seat. What do you do? Agree with him? After all, he is your boss. Do you mumble something unintelligible and excuse yourself from the room? Or do you make it known that the numbers are wrong?

Facing Ethical Dilemmas

That scenario is among the numerous ethical dilemmas that employees at MCI—the reconstituted telecommunications company rising from the ashes of scandal-ridden WorldCom Inc.—are asked to confront in training sessions these days. So far, more than 3,000 persons at the 55,000- employee company have either undergone the training or are registered for it, reports Richard Breeden, former chairman of the Securities and Exchange Commission and president of his own consulting firm in Greenwich, Conn. Breeden, who was appointed corporate monitor by the bankruptcy court, is overseeing MCI's return to respectability.

"If people just remembered what their mothers taught them, it would carry them a long way," Breeden says. "But one of the things about ethical decisions is that they can come up quickly. In a business environment, you don't have time talk to your mother or your minister."

Training programs like the one at MCI today teach employees what they should have learned at home or in Sunday school. In addition, they emphasize what many ethicists and corporate reformers increasingly recognize: that most of the scandals that have beset Corporate America have deep roots in dysfunctional organizations, the dictates of which too frequently overwhelm an employee's better angels.

It should come as no surprise. The social critic and religious philosopher Reinhold Niebuhr anticipated the fundamental causes of recent business skullduggery in the 1930s, when he wrote *Moral Man and Immoral Society*. In the book, Niebuhr argues that insidious institutions and peer pressures can compel otherwise honorable individuals to engage in sinister acts and perpetuate injustice.

A Climate of Corruption

As the past couple of years have shown, the outsized financial frauds that have landed top executives in jail, driven companies into bankruptcy, deprived investors of their life savings and thrown the financial markets into turmoil were aided and abetted by intelligent and law-abiding citizens.

Indeed, experts in the fields of law, accounting and business ethics say that one crucial lesson to be learned from the fraud at Enron Corp., WorldCom, HealthSouth Corp., Global Crossing Inc., Adelphia Communications, Tyco International and Xerox Corp., among other egregious examples, is how easy it is for otherwise honest people to be swept up in a climate of corruption.

"We have learned the same thing again and again: financial fraud does not start with dishonesty," says Michael Young, a partner at the New York law firm of Willkie, Farr & Gallagher. "Your boss doesn't come to you and say, 'Let's do some financial fraud.' Fraud occurs because the culture has become infected. It spreads like an unstoppable virus."

Brian Brinig, a San Diego attorney, agrees. "Virtually everybody I see gets up and goes to work in the morning trying to do a good job," he says. "But at some point, people lose sight of the forest for the trees. The pressures of achieving short-term goals cause them to become short-sighted in relation to longer-term moral and ethical objectives."

Fraud Is Widespread

And it is not just the high-profile publicized cases where cooking the books occurs. Accounting and financial fraud, unfortunately, have been far more widespread than just the celebrated scandals. The U.S. General Accounting Office (GAO), the watchdog agency of the U.S. Congress, noted [in 2002] that 689 companies restated their earnings between 1997 and 2002. While many of the restatements were done for technical reasons or because of rule changes, the cumulative effect was nonetheless stunning: all told, the restatements resulted in losses of close to $100 billion in market capitalization, the GAO found. "That's a lot of money evaporated," remarks Toby Bishop, president of the Association of Chief Fraud Examiners (ACFE), headquartered in Austin, Texas.

It also helps explain why highly publicized legal action by state attorneys general and the U.S. Justice Department have been on the rise. So, too, are costly class-action lawsuits. The 217 cases of private securities litigation brought during 2002 represented a hike of 17 percent compared with the year before, according to a PriceWaterhouseCoopers study. . . .

Crimes by Married Couples

When it comes to white-collar criminals, husbands and wives can also turn out to be partners in crime.

Spouses have banded together to swindle insurance companies, take kickbacks for inside-trading tips and launder tens of thousands of dollars.

But those who commit white-collar crimes—which often involve high-ranking employees engaged in fraud for financial gain—face additional woes if they team with a spouse. Prosecutors can find it easier to get a confession by leveraging one spouse against another. Marriages can fray under the pressure of a lengthy and uncertain federal investigation. Families with children face questions about how to provide care if both are sentenced to prison.

And while some marriages can be destroyed when allegations are leveled against them, other relationships are strengthened as spouses band together to face the social and career-crippling stigma of a criminal charge. . . .

Stephanie Armour, USA Today, *May 23, 2007.*

Rewarding the Guilty

By all accounts, the corporate swamps that serve as a breeding ground for fraud have two common characteristics: overly aggressive targets for financial performance and a can-do culture that does not tolerate failure. It is not uncommon, moreover, for what becomes a massive fraud to start out small.

"There's an expectation that, 'We just need a small amount of additional revenue or earnings—or both—and with a minor adjustment, we can meet Wall Street's estimates,'" observes

Paul Regan, president of Hemming Morse in San Francisco and a forensic accountant involved in financial fraud investigations for 30 years. "So people reduce a judgment account, like the allowance for bad debts."

"There's always the expectation that next quarter will be okay," he adds. "People say, 'We can patch things up.' But the next quarter comes along, and they've got to do a little bit more. Pretty soon, it gets to be very noticeable. But you can't go back. So that's how they get trapped."

At the same time that people are striving frantically to meet unrealistic Wall Street earnings projections in order to keep buoying the company's stock price—that holy grail of the corporate world—the culture demands and rewards success. Numerous investigations into financial fraud, notes Breeden, have identified the "tone at the top" as a root cause. Adds Regan: "In a lot of these scandals, the CEO is a very charismatic guy. Sometimes it's a 'celebrity CEO,' like Ken Lay at Enron."

And then there is the CEO whom Regan describes as "a dominant, over-powering bully who won't take 'no' for an answer." ACFE's Bishop asserts that this take-no-prisoners leader bears all the earmarks of a psychopath: among other qualities, he—it will usually be a man—is megalomaniacal, glib and superficial. This personality shows no remorse, is by nature deceitful and manipulative, impulsive and has a need for excitement. "These are people who are focused more on the ends than the means, and do whatever it takes to accomplish their objectives," Bishop says.

Consider WorldCom. There, says Breeden, former CEO Bernie Ebbers "scoffed at ethics and controls. He communicated the message that 'real men only worry about revenue growth.' People who didn't were pansies. The people who got promotions were not the ones who told the truth, but people who claimed credit for things they didn't do, twisted reality and promised things without worrying about whether they could deliver."

A Panoply of Controls

Experts applaud the panoply of newly enacted controls, such as [the] Sarbanes-Oxley [Act] and corporate governance reforms, designed to put an end to such practices—and put more white-collar criminals behind bars. Particularly welcome are such avenues for whistleblowers as toll-free telephone numbers, Web sites and an ombudsman to field reports of fraud, scares and assorted ethical violations.

But Bishop, for one, would like to have seen better training and education programs insisted upon in the law. "If a CFO instructs a corporate comptroller to book a certain entry which is misstating results," Bishop says, "the comptroller needs to know it's a crime—not just aggressive accounting—and that he should not be aiding and abetting in a felony."

The abiding belief that better training and education are essential to snuffing out a climate of corruption has taken hold at MCI. The CEO and top management have signed an ethics pledge and can be fired for violating their oath of duty. The company's newly minted code of ethics, "The Way We Work," is etched on the reverse side of everyone's identification badge; similarly, signage proclaiming the code are on display throughout the company.

Employees by the hundreds are taking classroom and on-line training courses, learning the basic responsibilities required by laws like Sarbanes-Oxley and the Securities Act of 1934. MCI staffers are learning the fundamentals of accounting rules, as well, and are being admonished to take them seriously and to spot the most common methods by which they can be circumvented. In addition, there are now classes using case studies and role-playing to reinforce ethical behavior. . . .

Bad Behavior Becomes Ingrained

Mark A. Zorko, CFO Partner at Tatum Partners, recalls the ethical issues he confronted when he was brought in during the mid-1990s as the CFO of a $240 million publicly held electronics manufacturing firm. A revived board had ousted the previous management following the discovery of significant fraud. So Zorko and his finance team had the support of the new leadership in deciding how to resolve the situation.

But, as Zorko found, "You can get rid of the top guys, but there's still likely to be lingering bad behavior." People thought they were doing the right things, he says, when they were given incentives to make their numbers. Pricing problems, inventory mis-management and shipping discrepancies continued. After a couple of years of having such behavior condoned, these practices had become ingrained.

"As we brought a new finance team in and began draining the pond, we found deeper problems, caused by a lack of good financial management and misguided incentives," Zorko remembers. "We had situations, for example, where we disagreed about inventory valuation. Is that bad judgment or fraud? When I see [a lot] of dust on boxes of electronic parts for instance, I have a tough time accepting a plant manager's view on their full value." Zorko says the business was worse than had been initially envisioned. Eventually, it was liquidated.

"Accounting irregularities never occur in a vacuum—these things start with business operations failing to meet expectations," he says. "Some companies have resorted to trying to fix their problems with magic pencils.

"You can have management that legally might not fit the context of what fraud encompasses, but is tantamount to it," he adds. Cleaning it up "still means changing the habits and behavior of an organization—to go from bad to good or good to better can take a lot of coaching. It's easy to underestimate how much time it can take."

Periodical Bibliography

Sam E. Antar   "A Fraudster's Thoughts," July 9, 2005.
                            www.whitecollarfraud.com.

Kathleen F. Brickey   "In Enron's Wake: Corporate Executives on
                            Trial," *Journal of Criminal Law and Criminology*, Winter 2006.

Pamela H. Bucy,   "Why Do They Do It? The Motives, Mores and
Elizabeth P. Formby,   Character of White Collar Criminals," *St. John's
Marc S. Raspanti and   Law Review*, Spring 2008.
Kathryn E. Rooney

Maureen Duffy-Lewis   "Dancing in the Rain: Who Is Your Partner in
and Daniel B. Garrie   the Corporate Boardroom?" *John Marshall
                            Journal of Computer & Information Law*, Spring
                            2008.

Drew Feeley   "Personality, Environment, and the Causes of
                            White-Collar Crime," *Law and Psychology Review*, vol. 30, 2006.

Michelle S. Jacobs   "Loyalty's Reward—a Felony Conviction: Recent Prosecutions of High-Status Female Offenders," *Fordham Urban Law Journal*, March
                            2006.

Steven D. Levitt   "White-Collar Crime Writ Small: A Case Study
                            of Bagels, Donuts, and the Honor System,"
                            American Economic Review, May 2006.

Peter Monaghan   "The White-Collar Criminal as Thug,"
                            Chronicle of Higher Education, September 28,
                            2007.

Walt Pavlo   "Lies, Fraud, and Felony," *Industrial Engineer*,
                            August 2007.

Herbert Sherman and   "Take the Money and Run," *Journal of the International Academy for Case Studies*, March–
Daniel J. Rowley   April 2007.

OPPOSING
VIEWPOINTS®
SERIES

CHAPTER 3

Is White-Collar Crime Appropriately Punished?

Chapter Preface

In 2004, one of the largest energy companies in the world, the Enron Corporation, filed for bankruptcy. Enron chairman Kenneth Lay and other members of its board of directors were accused of insider trading and falsifying quarterly reports by billions of dollars. Days before the bankruptcy filing, Lay and other executives sold their stock shares, depleting the retirement savings of hundreds of employees. The scandal caused a national outrage. Politicians vowed to bring big business under tighter regulations. The resulting lawsuits brought down not just Enron but led to the dissolution of Enron's accounting firm, Arthur Andersen, for deliberately committing fraudulent irregularities and artificially inflating Enron's stock price for months.

The Enron scandal was a crippling financial disaster that did irreparable damage to the reputation of the American corporation. Thousands of employees and stockholders lost their life savings. Several social critics observed that this instance of corporate duplicity had inarguably caused more widespread suffering than any murder spree in history.

Yet although Lay and Andersen chairman Jeffrey Skilling were found guilty of their crimes, neither man served any prison time. The death of Lay in 2004 prevented both the government and individuals from seeking punitive damages from his estate. No individual at the company or among the legislators in Washington who had allowed Enron's excesses to go on for years without critical scrutiny resigned or was fired for inaction or for failing to monitor the relaxed regulations that had enabled the fraud to occur. There was no suggestion on the part of the media, the litigators, the victims, or the general public that any of the executives responsible should be sentenced to years in maximum security penitentiaries alongside street criminals.

In another historic example of corporate negligence, it was revealed in February 2009 that the U.S. company Peanut Corporation had either knowingly or negligently allowed contaminated peanut butter to be sold on store shelves, causing hundreds of people to fall ill and killing at least six as a result of salmonella poisoning. Although government investigations ensued and civil lawsuits were filed, few in the media suggested that those responsible should pay with their lives. By contrast, in 2007 China executed the head of its food and drug safety agency for taking bribes that had allowed animal feed tainted with melamine to be used in baby formula sold on the open market. While some Americans regarded this as overly harsh if not barbaric, others claimed that it was simply justice in action.

There is considerable evidence to support the perception that white-collar criminals tend to be underpunished and that they even get away with their crimes. People with sufficient money to commit financial crimes can generally afford to make bail or hire the best legal counsel. They are also likelier to have powerful allies within the system itself.

Yet in the wake of the Enron scandal and the mortgage and banking crises of 2008, which damaged the reputation of the financial industry, some complain that heightened scrutiny has also left corporations open to reverse discrimination. They argue that news media sources and federal prosecutors attempt to win the public's attention and approval by making examples of certain corporations by inflating their transgressions or singling out political enemies while giving other offenders a free pass.

The question of whether the prison system is an efficient deterrent to corporate crime also remains the subject of heated debate. Some contend that having executives pay back what they owe in exchange for deferred sentencing is better for the economy and a more fitting penance. Others retort that fines and prison time should not necessarily be exclusive. And still others believe that all punishments should be uniform to offenders regardless of their social status.

The authors of the following viewpoints offer a wide range of dissenting views on what constitutes the appropriate punishment for white-collar criminals and whether ultimately any punishment can be enough.

> *"From an honest businessman's perspective, the most worrisome thing about the Enron case was the jurors' unconcealed prejudice and the court's lack of concern about it."*

White-Collar Criminals Are Unfairly Punished

Nicole Gelinas

Despite their affluence and status, white-collar criminals often face a stacked deck in the courtroom, according to Nicole Gelinas, the author of the following viewpoint. Gelinas argues that business is based on honest predictions that are sometimes wrong rather than fraudulent. Gelinas also notes that due to the complexity of accounting, jurors tend to be openly biased against white-collar offenders.

Nicole Gelinas is the Searle Freedom Trust Fellow at the Manhattan Institute and a contributing editor of City Journal. *She has written analysis and opinion articles for numerous publications, including the* New York Times, Wall Street Journal, *the* Los Angeles Times, *and the* Boston Herald.

Nicole Gelinas, "Criminalizing Capitalism," *City Journal*, vol. 18, Winter 2008. Copyright © The Manhattan Institute. Reproduced by permission.

As you read, consider the following questions:

1. According to the author, what two advantages are enjoyed by prosecutors over defense attorneys?

2. What are two recommendations Gelinas cites as methods of mitigating personal losses in future financial crises like the Enron scandal?

3. What does the author use as an example of a public statement by a CEO that some critics would consider fraudulent?

Another asset bubble has burst, this one in American real estate and its financing. Precariously structured mortgage investments teeter and fall, bringing corporate titans down and crushing investor confidence. Financial firms, led by Citigroup and Merrill Lynch, have miscalculated and mismanaged key risks and seen more than $100 billion in shareholder assets vanish. Mortgage-related turmoil has roiled markets, with economists and ordinary Americans fearing that lending woes and a protracted home-price decline could trigger a recession.

It wasn't supposed to be this way. After Enron imploded six years ago, Congress and President [George W.] Bush enacted the Sarbanes-Oxley law, which aimed to reform corporate practices and prevent future market surprises. The law imposed new regulations on corporations and their executives, as well as new criminal sanctions for corporate wrongdoing under both the new law and existing ones. "How can you measure the value of knowing that company books are sounder than they were before?" asked sponsor Michael Oxley, defending the law. "Of no more overnight bankruptcies with the employees and retirees left holding the bag? No more disruption to entire sectors of the economy?"

But in the end, Sarbanes-Oxley has just made it easier for ambitious government attorneys to criminalize bad business judgment and complex accounting in hindsight. Further, in their focus on strengthening legal enforcement, the feds have passed up opportunities to create commonsense protections for investors. Worse still, the government has instilled investors with false confidence by implying that they can rely on prosecutors, not prudence, to protect their market holdings. Now the housing and mortgage meltdown—which could hurt the economy far more than Enron did—is reminding investors that no law or regulation can protect them from economic disruption. . . .

A Brief History of Prosecutions

Wall Street prosecutions weren't born with Sarbanes-Oxley. As prominent white-collar defense attorney Stan Arkin says, prestigious law firms regarded criminal-defense practices as unsavory 40 years ago, but the increased threat of white-collar prosecutions eventually led almost all of them to offer such services. Many in the financial world first understood the acute risks in the 1980s, when Rudy Giuliani—then the U.S. attorney for the Southern District of New York, which includes Wall Street—ordered three investment bankers arrested in their offices or homes, one of them in handcuffs, on suspicion of insider trading, though two of the three cases against them were later dropped.

Also during, the 1980s, financial firms realized that if they didn't cooperate quickly with government investigators, their investors and assets could disappear just as quickly, and even cooperation wasn't a guarantee of survival. In what observers hailed as a far-reaching agreement, Drexel Burnham Lambert, junk-bond king Michael Milken's investment company, cooperated with the feds, waiving some attorney-client privileges and agreeing to dismiss Milken in order to fend off securities-fraud charges. (Drexel, reeling from both the government investigation and the loss of Milken's business, soon sold off its best assets anyway.) To get dirt on Milken, the feds also charged five principals at investment firm Princeton/Newport, a Milken trading partner, with racketeering, tax fraud, and other crimes. Even before the principals' convictions—the most serious among them later overturned—the investigation and the threat to seize assets under antiracketeering law terrified investors and spelled the firm's demise.

After the tech bubble burst in 2000, New York attorney general [AG] Eliot Spitzer pursued investment banks, mutual-fund companies, and insurance companies with headline-grabbing intensity—cratering their stock prices, exacting expensive settlements merely by threatening to prosecute, and reminding CEOs how much power an ambitious AG wields. For instance, in 2002, Spitzer went after Merrill Lynch for pushing its customers to buy wildly overvalued stock in companies that were paying Merrill hefty investment-banking fees at the same time. Hemorrhaging market value, Merrill cowered when Spitzer announced that its actions were "corrupt" and "maybe criminal." The firm swiftly settled, agreeing to pay a $100 million fine—to the government, not to investors—and to change its business practices. Spitzer employed similar tactics and made even more egregious public statements in order to pressure other firms—notably AIG, forcing the insurance giant to fire longtime CEO and chairman Hank Greenberg, even though, as Spitzer biographer Brooke Masters writes, zero evidence had linked him to the company's alleged accounting misdeeds.

Prosecutorial Advantages

Prosecutors have eagerly adopted all these techniques. Princeton/Newport, for example, was a direct precursor to Arthur Andersen, Enron's auditor, which failed in 2002 because it couldn't withstand an obstruction-of-justice indictment; the Supreme Court eventually overturned Andersen's subsequent conviction, but the storied firm's doors stay shuttered. [In the fall of 2007], a health-care company, WellCare, watched three-quarters of its market value vaporize after government investigators invaded its offices without saying why.

And today, firms routinely waive attorney-client privilege and turn over evidence against their workers in order to protect themselves from even the threat of indictment.

White-collar prosecutors have, moreover, long enjoyed two advantages over defense attorneys. The first is what lawyers call the "white-collar rationale," under which courts are reluctant to impose limitations on prosecutors' tactics, particularly before indictment, in everything from gathering physical evidence to interviewing witnesses. The white-collar rationale exists because courts see prosecuting white-collar crimes as unusually difficult. For other kinds of crime—homicide, for example—it's obvious that something illegal has occurred, and the question is straightforward: Who did it? But for white-collar crime, while it's often clear who acted—a CEO tells the public that his company's prospects are good, but the company later fails; a debt underwriter tells a short-term investor that a piece of debt is worth $50 million, but later can't find a price for more than $20 million; a trader chats with a company's officer and then sells shares of the company's stock just before the price plummets—it's unclear whether the action is a crime or not.

Wayne State law professor Peter Henning writes in the *University of Pittsburgh Law Review* that "the acceptance of the white-collar rationale . . . to permit the government to seek incriminating statements from participants, and to limit the privilege against self-incrimination, means that the cases will continue to be decided generally in favor of the government." Baker Botts defense lawyer J. Bradley Bennett says that "while the most obvious result of federal law enforcement's aggressive pursuit of white-collar prosecutions has been the criminalization of conduct" formerly treated as civil violations, a subtler shift is that "the government has dramatically changed the way in which it investigates and prosecutes business crime"—using search warrants that effectively shut down small securities firms, for example, before those firms can hire criminal lawyers.

Another reason for the white-collar rationale is that judges often consider wealthy defendants fully able to take care of themselves. This points to prosecutors' second advantage: predisposition against executives during the trial itself. "For many judges and jurors, what goes on in an executive suite may just as well be happening on Mars," says University of Illinois law professor Larry Ribstein. "Newspapers, films, and other media sources . . . portray corporate executives as selfish, greedy, and irresponsible." So if a trial reveals, say, that a firm's chief accountant questioned a particular valuation method and that the CEO then directed other employees to challenge the accountant, a jury may see the CEO's defiance as criminal conspiracy, not normal corporate give-and-take. . . .

The Complexities of Accounting

From an honest businessman's perspective, the most worrisome thing about the Enron case was the jurors' unconcealed prejudice and the court's lack of concern about it. One juror wrote on a pretrial questionnaire: "I think [Jeff Skilling and Ken Lay] probably knew they were breaking the law."

Another wrote that the "collapse was due to greed and mismanagement." A third said that "pure greed" motivated all CEOs and that "some get caught and some don't," adding: "Anyone that takes home the salaries and bonuses and the stuff they have, they got to be greedy." These prejudices somehow didn't bother the court, which had already refused the defense's request to move the trial from Houston, where Enron-related emotions ran high.

After the trial, it became clear that some jurors didn't even understand what they had convicted the two defendants of doing. Describing how he had reached the guilty verdict, Delgado said: "To say you didn't know what was going on in your own company was not the right thing." Another juror, Dana Fernandez, said that if Lay and Skilling "didn't know, they should have found out somehow what was going on." But the

What Sentence Is Fair?

Bernard J. Ebbers, the former chairman of *WorldCom* who was convicted of masterminding an $11 billion accounting fraud that bankrupted the company, was sentenced to 25 years in prison.

Because Mr. Ebbers is 63, some have contended that the sentence amounts to a life term. Likewise, John J. Rigas, the 80-year-old founder of *Adelphia Communications*, was sentenced to 15 years.

"You have to ask yourself whether the proof in these cases warrants such a sentence," said Otto G. Obermaier, a former United States attorney in Manhattan, who had been an aggressive prosecutor of white-collar crimes when he ran the office from 1989 to 1993. "Ebbers's sentence moved the goal posts pretty far back. You can describe it as a pendulum switch, but it is an overreaction." . . .

Depending on the length of the sentence, both men could be incarcerated in a maximum-security prison like Attica.

No lawyer is suggesting that white-collar criminals not serve time. Rather, lawyers and jurists are asking what the appropriate sentence is for white-collar crimes relative to punishments for other crimes in a post-Enron world.

Andrew Ross Sorkin,
New York Times, *September 16, 2005.*

burden of the government's case was to prove beyond reasonable doubt that Lay and Skilling had engineered a conspiratorial fraud. If they didn't know about the conspiracy—regardless of whether they should have known about it—the jury should have found them not guilty. (To be fair, the judge may have improperly instructed the jury on this point.). . .

Criminalizing Mistakes

The most recent round of spectacular business misjudgments raises the question of what happens, in this new era, when a CEO misses a warning sign in his company that later becomes painfully obvious. In the mortgage debacle, the world's most sophisticated financiers, as well as ratings agents who signaled that it was prudent to invest in ever-riskier mortgage-backed securities, seemed to believe that housing prices would keep going up, in large part thanks to cheap and easy credit. Bankers and executives also thought that careful engineering—and, yes, complex accounting and financing—would insulate these securities from precipitous losses even if the housing market did tank eventually. Were their huge and unexpected losses the results of poor internal controls? After all, didn't CEOs, who signed off on such controls, know that their employees, pursuing big bonuses, had an incentive to take bigger risks than shareholders might have recognized? And didn't the CEOs realize that their opaque models for structuring and valuing these securities were disastrously vulnerable to error? Or did the losses simply result from spectacular misjudgments—unavoidable from time to time in a free-market economy?

With foreclosures piling up because borrowers and lenders both made overoptimistic assumptions about the housing market, the government is already using its implicit prosecutorial power to bully banks with a role in the crisis. When treasury secretary Henry Paulson, with President Bush's backing, "encourages" mortgage lenders to freeze interest rates on subprime mortgages so that some borrowers won't face foreclosure, those banks understand that they'd better take his words to heart: the next government caller may not be so encouraging.

It would be no surprise if an ambitious state attorney general or U.S. attorney seized on citizen and media anger and hauled some executives into the courtroom, not only over internal controls but over possible conflicts of interest. In fact, New York AG Andrew Cuomo, Spitzer's successor, has already subpoenaed Wall Street banks, including Merrill Lynch and Bear Stearns, to find out what was going on when they structured and sold mortgage-backed securities; his counterparts in other states aren't far behind. For example, did bankers ever discuss the risks of such securities among themselves but neglect to mention those risks to potential investors? The FBI has also launched a criminal investigation of 14 banks, looking into possible insider trading, accounting fraud, and disclosure omissions surrounding the mortgage crisis.

There's also the issue of public statements and omissions. Countrywide Financial CEO Angelo Mozilo told investors that he expected his firm to turn a profit last quarter despite the mortgage meltdown—the worst crisis that his company, until recently the nation's largest mortgage lender, had ever faced. Instead, the bank reported another hefty loss. Was Mozilo's comment just optimism, however irrational in hindsight? Or was it a fraudulent lie, meriting prison? Similarly, many observers say that banks should have disclosed clearly to shareholders that they might have multibillion-dollar obligations, in certain market conditions, to outside investment partnerships holding subprime securities. But no company can clearly disclose every potential obligation in every conceivable market condition; the resulting paperwork would be too voluminous for any investor to digest. Showing how easy it is to paint gray areas of disclosure black, however, *New York Times* business columnist Floyd Norris recently mentioned "signs that banks were either lying about their results or were taking large risks that were not fully disclosed." The CEOs were lying . . . or they were lying. Not a tough choice for a jury. . . .

Limiting Risk

Because perfect knowledge and disclosure of risk, and perfectly rational responses to available disclosure, aren't attainable, what might be done to mitigate personal losses in future crises? One partial solution is for the government to put checks on a normally beneficial force: natural optimism. For retirement savings, the feds should use the tax code to discourage investors from putting all their eggs into one basket. Though investors should be free to speculate on the next big thing, they shouldn't be free to do so in retirement accounts like 401(k)s and IRAs, accorded favorable tax treatment by the government. Perhaps Enron's worst sin was what a human-resources director said at a 1999 company assembly, when an employee asked, "Should we invest all of our 401(k) in Enron stock?" "Absolutely!" the director responded. "Don't you guys agree?" she added to the enthusiastic Lay and Skilling, who stood nearby. The result: many workers lost not only their jobs but much of their retirement savings.

The feds should thus revive a failed Enron-era proposal banning companies from allowing employees to invest more than 10 percent of in-house retirement savings in their companies' stock. Congress should also prohibit the owner of any independent 401(k) or IRA from investing more than 15 percent of retirement assets in one company or 20 percent in one industry. (Investors could still do so elsewhere, of course.) And Congress should continue to prevent people from using their 401(k) accounts to invest in their homes, despite suggestions that lifting the ban would prop up the housing market. Housing assets, just as vulnerable to market bubbles as stocks are, already make up too large a percentage of Americans' savings.

As the economy heads into a possible downturn, calls will grow for someone to pay for the pain of another burst bubble—and for yet more onerous rules, regulations, and prosecutions of businesses to prevent future crises. But no government mandate or punishment, however harsh, will stop companies and markets from being imperfect collections of fallible human beings. At the end of a decade of financial surprises, that may be the most enduring lesson of all.

> *"Even with record-level collections of more than $1.5 billion, the U.S. Department of Justice brought in only 3.3 percent of all criminal debt on the books [in 2006]."*

White-Collar Criminals Rarely Repay Their Debts

Ross Todd

Even when white-collar criminals are caught red-handed, their victims usually see little to no financial restitution, according to Ross Todd, the author of the following viewpoint. Citing independent statistics, Todd argues that not only do those guilty of most million- and billion-dollar crimes wind up paying nothing at all in the way of financial penalties but that, due to the inherent complexities of the legal system, efforts by Justice Department officials to secure payments from indicted criminals, even minimal amounts, wind up costing more money to process and collect and disburse than the sums themselves.

Ross Todd is a regular contributor to American Lawyer *and other journals.*

As you read, consider the following questions:

1. According to the author, what are two obstacles faced by prosecutors in trying to turn restitution judgments into actual cash for victims?

2. What are three "reasonable explanations" offered by Department of Justice officials, as cited by Todd, for their failure to guarantee that victims of white-collar crimes are not "being compensated for their losses to the fullest extent possible"?

3. What are two reasons the author cites that make collection of financial restitution difficult?

Technically speaking, Jay Jones is more than $1 billion in the red. Five years ago [in 2002], when he pleaded guilty to conspiracy, federal district court judge Sven Erik Holmes ordered him to pay $1,089,636,980 to victims of the fraud that he committed at Tulsa's Commercial Financial Services, Inc. CFS bought bad credit card debt and collected on accounts that other companies had written off—but when CFS's collections dipped, Jones funneled bad debt into a separate company, fraudulently propping up the value of CFS bonds.

Today, though, it's as though Jones's debts have been written off. The government seized more than $4.4 million worth of his assets before he went to prison. Now, with monthly income of about $1,500 in Social Security and $1,000 for odd jobs he takes for the law firm that once defended him, the ridiculously unattainable $1.1 billion might as well be a trillion. "Honestly, from my standpoint," Jones says matter-of-factly with a Northern Oklahoma drawl, "if it would have been $400,000 or $500,000, it would have scared me more than $1 billion."

In fact, Jones hasn't paid a cent toward restitution since his release in January [2007] after three-and-a-half years in prison, followed by six months split between a halfway house and home detention. Adding insult to mega-injury, if Jones started to make small payments, it would cost more for the CFS estate to administer the distributions than Jones can afford to pay.

Jones is just one of the many corporate fraudsters who will never repay the debt they've been deemed to owe their victims. Judges have handed down some staggering restitution orders in both high-profile and obscure cases during the past five years: E. Kirk Shelton and Walter Forbes both owe $3.275 billion in the Cendant Corporation case prosecuted by the New Jersey U.S. attorney's office, and former executives of Michigan mortgage company MCA Financial Corp. owe as much as $256 million in restitution. Of the defendants prosecuted under the banner of the Corporate Fraud Task Force, at least 25 people face more than $7 million in restitution debts (in some cases jointly and severally with their codefendants). Those debts are based on documented, direct losses by victims.

But how much of the money will be collected? The Jones case is a fairly representative example. The government seized Jones's assets (including an unfinished house valued at more than $600,000, a 1998 Chevy pickup truck, and a 2000 Cadillac sedan) before he was released from prison. "The government did a pretty good job of hanging on to everything I have," Jones says, except for his clothes and an old guitar. Still, that sum was just more than 4 percent of the total restitution Judge Holmes ordered. And that's not too far off the national average according to the U.S. Attorneys' Annual Statistical Report for fiscal year 2006: even with record-level collections of more than $1.5 billion, the U.S. Department of Justice brought in only 3.3 percent of all criminal debt on the books last year.

A Growing Imbalance

The responsibility to enforce fines and restitution in federal cases rests with financial litigation units—teams of data entry clerks and collection specialists headed up by an assistant U.S.

attorney from the civil division in each of the 93 U.S. attorney's offices. Prosecutors face many obstacles in trying to turn restitution judgments into actual cash for victims, according to information gathered from court filings, congressional studies, and discussions with about 30 lawyers and victims involved in white-collar fraud cases. Some white-collar defendants don't actually have much money, particularly those convicted of operating sham companies or Ponzi schemes [investment scams]. Of those who do, some take advantage of the time it takes to investigate and prosecute corporate fraud by transferring and hiding assets in the meantime. Sometimes the award is so preposterously huge that even a decent-sized collection doesn't put a dent in it.

Senators from both sides of the aisle, including North Dakota Democrat Byron Dorgan and Maine Republican Susan Collins, have asked the Government Accountability Office (GAO) to look into the collection of criminal debts, the fines and restitution owed to the government and to third parties since 2001. According to several assistant U.S. attorneys who handle collection cases, the congressional scrutiny has pushed prosecutors to think beyond the initial conviction and coordinate their efforts with financial litigation units well before sentencing to go after criminal assets. Yet the balance of uncollected fines and restitution continues to grow—up by $4.3 billion to $45.7 billion for fiscal year 2006. More than 75 percent of that amount consists of restitution owed to victims. Going forward, additional convictions mean more restitution judgments, but without a significant uptick in collections, these awards will seem increasingly meaningless to victims, criminals, and the public.

No matter how much restitution—or how little—the government may ultimately collect from a criminal, first it has to calculate the size of the award and who should receive it. In a corporate fraud case, victims are typically identified by investigating agencies, such as the Federal Bureau of Investigation or the Securities and Exchange Commission. After a conviction, a probation officer presents the court with a presentence report, which includes a summary of the criminal's finances and a collection of statements from victims about the financial and emotional impact of the crime. In some cases, judges order restitution as a lump sum payable at sentencing, plus a monthly amount to be paid after release from prison. In other cases, the whole amount comes due in full at judgment.

The 7 Percent Problem

The federal law that governs restitution assures that in most big-dollar frauds there will be big-dollar restitution judgments. The Mandatory Victims Restitution Act of 1996, the federal law that governs how the courts determine restitution in most white-collar fraud cases, says that judges "shall order restitution to each victim in the full amount of each victim's losses as determined by the court and without consideration of the economic circumstances of the defendant." The law clearly had an effect on the overall balance of criminal debt on the books as well. The U.S. attorneys' annual statistical report shows the total amount of criminal debt owed increased from about $6 billion in 1995—the last year before restitution amounts were governed by the new law—to nearly $46 billion in 2006.

For at least two decades, the GAO has highlighted problems in collecting fines and restitution in multiple reports to Congress. Each year U.S. attorneys report criminal debts as well as collections made on those debts. In 2001 the GAO found that an average of only 7 percent of all fines and restitution in a five-year span was collected; 66 percent of the uncollected money was restitution to victims outside of the government. In a follow-up report in 2004, the GAO found that the average rate for collections had dipped to 4 percent.

In a 2005 report, the GAO focused on restitution in a selection of white-collar cases at the request of Senator Dorgan.

The study found that only 7 percent of the total restitution amounts were collected, even in cases where records indicated criminals had millions in assets prior to sentencing. (All information that could identify individual criminals was withheld from the study.) The 2005 report concluded that without a strategic plan to address the problem of criminal debt collections, the Department of Justice could not guarantee "that offenders are not benefiting from ill-gotten gains and that innocent victims are being compensated for their losses to the fullest extent possible." (Such a strategic plan was delivered to Congress in summer 2005; it set goals to improve Justice's ability to identify assets, make collections, and track outstanding debt while raising the possibility of bringing in private collection agencies.)

Justice officials argue that there are reasonable explanations for the eye-popping statistics cited by the GAO. Fines and restitution can stay on the books for 20 years after a criminal's release from prison. Debt lingers on Justice's books until it's paid, the statute of limitations expires, the debtor dies, or the court approves its removal—a resource-consuming process that most prosecutors don't spend time pursuing.

In comments included in the response sections of the 2005 GAO report, Mary Beth Buchanan, then director of the Executive Office for United States Attorneys, pointed out that although Congress gave Justice a new mandate to collect restitution on behalf of victims under the 1996 restitution law, it allotted no additional resources to the U.S. attorneys offices to carry out that work. Legislation sponsored by Dorgan and endorsed by Justice is now pending in the Senate. The bill would give prosecutors the power to freeze assets preconviction in cases where a big restitution award could be in the offing.

The Price of Collection

Sometimes what appears as a win on paper for prosecutors turns out to be a big headache. Take the $1.1 billion restitution judgment in Jay Jones's case: While Jones was in prison in late 2003, the Federal Bureau of Prisons sent a check for $25 (from his quarterly prison earnings of less than $40) payable to the federal court clerk in Tulsa. It was a mistake: The judge had ordered the $1.1 billion restitution payable to the bankruptcy trustee of Jones's company, CFS, so the check should not have been made out to the court or sent there. Through the mix-up, the judge learned that each time the trustee in the case pays out, it costs up to $4,000 to update the list of victims and cut checks.

The victims in the CFS case are people and institutions who hold CFS bonds and other company obligations. These notes can easily be transferred and sold, which makes tracking down their holders a difficult task. "The cost of making a distribution of small quarterly payments would result in no money whatsoever going to the victims," wrote Judge Holmes in a November 2003 supplemental order. "In fact, any such distribution would actually cause a net loss to the victims, since the administrative costs to effect a distribution must be deducted from the proceeds." The judge clarified that Jones still owed the victims their due, but resolved that there was no point in compounding the victims' losses with these small checks. If Jones were somehow to get enough money to make a dent in the restitution award, he would have to pay—but as things stand today, he's essentially off the hook.

Although the sheer complexity of the debt proved to be an obstacle in the Jones case, in other cases the passage of time makes collection difficult. The case of the former chief executive officer of Countrymark Cooperative, Inc., David Swanson, went up and down on appeal multiple times under different sentencing regimes. More than ten years elapsed between the time Swanson fraudulently obtained more than $2.7 million from Countrymark, a regional farm cooperative in Indiana, and April 2007, when Judge Sarah Evans Barker's order for $2,193,452 in restitution was affirmed. But by then, prosecutors had lost the chance to collect on the only Swanson asset they'd been able to identify: his 60-acre farm. Swanson had already transferred the farm to his then wife, and on the eve of trial he took out a $1.6 million bank loan on the property. Assistant U.S. attorney Charles Goodloe, Jr., says that with the bank and the ex-wife holding claims to the farm, a judge ruled this summer [2007] that the government would not be able to use proceeds from the farm's sale to repay victims.

Sometimes there's nothing for prosecutors to go after in the first place. In Michigan, seven executives of MCA, a mortgage company, were convicted of accounting fraud, illegally boosting assets, revenues, and profits in hopes of cashing in on an initial public offering [IPO]. Joint and several restitution judgments ranged from $11 million to $256 million among the seven defendants, but prosecutors faced a hurdle in collecting: the company never cashed in on its intended initial public offering. The conspirators were living relatively modestly when their scheme came unhinged.

"[Collecting is] difficult, especially in a case like this where the fraud hadn't given them their big payoff yet," says Jennifer Gorland, an assistant U.S. attorney in Detroit who prosecuted MCA officials. An IPO would have meant more funds to distribute—but more victims and a bigger restitution, too, she notes.

Blood from a Stone

Even those criminals who did manage to cash out often plead poverty later on. "Let's see, what's the old line? 'I spent it on women, drinking, and drugs, and I blew the rest,'" says Patrick Layng, a former Chicago assistant U.S. attorney who prosecuted five executives of FLP Capital Group, Inc. "These are not the most fiscally responsible people." Between 1994 and 1998, the FLP defendants promised investors high returns on risk-free investments, but ultimately funneled the money they collected through corporate accounts back to themselves—and promptly spent it. The five owe restitution of more than $11 million. "Most of these [restitution judgments] are academic," says Layng, who now works as regional coordinator for Justice in Chicago. "[The victims] are not going to get their money back."

To many victims, that's hardly news. In February 2005 former Integrated Food Technologies chairman and CEO Jack Summers pleaded guilty to mail fraud, securities fraud, and selling unregistered securities; he was sentenced to 40 months in prison and ordered to pay $14,499,045.45 in restitution. A state judge in Mississippi had barred Summers from dealing in unregistered securities back in 1989 after he had routed to himself funds from a fish farm he ran. But with a new company, Integrated Food Technologies in Emmaus, Pennsylvania, Summers again sold unregistered stock to more than 850 people and again misappropriated company funds with help from an employee. With the company belly-up, victims have not seen a cent of restitution. "I guess the only restitution we have is that he's in jail," says Bruno Fiabane, who with his wife lost more than $500,000, according to court filings. . . . George Foradori, whose family also lost more than $300,000 in money invested with Summers, says he doesn't expect to see any restitution payments. "You can't get blood from a stone," says Foradori of Summers. "I've tried to put this all behind me."

And even when the government is able to collect restitution in big chunks, losses can be so large that full repayment remains a pipe dream. Former Cendant Corporation vice-chairman Shelton owes $3.275 billion in restitution stemming from his fraud conviction. Judge Alvin Thompson based the restitution order on settlements paid out by Cendant to settle shareholder suits and the $25 million Cendant paid for Shelton's defense. He has handed over cash and life insurance policies valued at $15 million. Prosecutors continue to pursue more than $20 million worth of property and accounts that

Shelton and his wife hold jointly. But even a complete liquidation of Shelton's assets would leave billions in owed restitution on the books. . . .

For his part, Jay Jones says he feels bad that he doesn't have enough income to pay restitution. But practically speaking, the only way he might be able to pay victims back is if he wins the lottery.

If he's lucky enough to come across that winning ticket, though, Jones knows what to do with it. "Chances are, I probably wouldn't hit the lottery," Jones quips. "But my daughter might."

> *"In addition to increases in the number of white-collar offenders being sentenced to prison, there is also evidence that the average prison length for some white-collar offenders has increased."*

White-Collar Criminals Often Do Prison Time

Brian K. Payne

Although many people believe that white-collar criminals rarely serve time in prison or do only minimal time in cushy "resort"- style facilities, Brian K. Payne, the author of the following viewpoint, argues that this is far from the truth. Citing recent prison statistics, Payne notes that prison time for white-collar offenders is on the rise.

Brian K. Payne is an associate professor in the Department of Sociology and Criminal Justice at Old Dominion University.

As you read, consider the following questions:

1. What are two reasons the author cites that make it difficult to know precisely how many white-collar criminals there are?

Brian K. Payne, *Incarcerating White-Collar Offenders*. Springfield, IL: Charles C. Thomas, 2003. © 2003 by Charles C. Thomas Publisher, Ltd. Reproduced by permission of Charles C. Thomas, Publisher, Ltd., Springfield, IL. Reproduced by permission.

2. In Payne's view, what three reasons seem to influence whether a white-collar offender goes to prison?

3. What are the four reasons the author uses to suggest that the number of white-collar incarcerations is on the rise?

A tough judge nicknamed Iron Mike for his stiff sentences once stated the following in imposing a white-collar criminal's sentence: "We must shed ourselves of the perception that white-collar criminals are 'good guys' who are too good to be in jail". Not long after this admonishment, the same judge pleaded guilty to tax evasion, was forced to quit his job, and was sent to prison for two months. In a similar case, a judge was sentenced to thirteen months in a medium security prison in which he met many individuals who were previously in his court. Some of the offenders with whom he was incarcerated actually had legal papers with the judge's name on it. Imagine how tough it would be to serve time with inmates whose sentences you imposed. Certainly, the protection of at-risk incarcerated white-collar criminals is one of the serious challenges jail and prison administrators face.

During the summer of 2000, 68-year-old Jai Coehlo was jailed in Rio de Janeiro pending the outcome of fraud and racketeering charges filed against him. What makes his case especially interesting is the nature of the charges. In particular, it was alleged that Coehlo, whose company supplied all prison food in Rio de Janeiro, committed fraudulent activities in fulfilling his contract to feed the prisoners covered under the contract. Reportedly, prison officials and prisoners alike complained about the horrible quality of the food. To protect the "fraudulent food man" from the inmates he had previously starved, Coehlo was segregated with older offenders who were not considered violent.

A number of highly profiled white-collar crime cases resulting in incarceration have been the focus of a great deal of media attention. Consider, for instance, the following cases:

- In November 1990, Michael Milken was sentenced to ten years in prison and ordered to pay $600 million in restitution and fines for fraudulent securities trading, conspiracy, and the junk bond operations he oversaw.

- In October 1989, Jim Bakker was sentenced to 45 years in prison and given a $500,000 fine after the evangelist defrauded his followers by diverting over $3.7 million from his ministry.

- Jake Butcher, former chairperson of United American Bank was sentenced to 20 years in prison after he plead guilty to fraud, income tax evasion, and conspiracy. Other "celebrity" white-collar inmates include G. Gordon Liddy, Jeb Magruder, former Illinois Governor Dan Walker, former Louisiana Governor Edwin Edwards, and a host of others. Along with these famous offenders, thousands of other senators, preachers, governors, doctors, and members of just about every profession imaginable have been imprisoned for misdeeds committed on the job.

However, because of difficulties defining white-collar crime and detecting these offenses, no one really knows precisely how many white-collar criminals there are. Even so, the 1980s and 1990s witnessed a significant increase in the number of white-collar offenders being sentenced to jail or prison, with the majority incarcerated in federal prisons though some are incarcerated in local jails and state prisons. As [journalist Ted] Thompson notes, prior to the 1980s, white-collar offenders asked, "Can I avoid prison?" Today, white-collar offenders are asking, "Can I get the top bunk?" . . .

Feeling the Pain

Not only do members of society want white-collar offenders to be punished, they also want them to "feel the pain" from their punishment. After one business was defrauded, the attorney for the defrauded business said of the offender "[he] is expected to do time, not at a country club federal prison where he can sharpen his tennis game, but at a medium high level security prison where he will live within a real criminal population". This comment is shallow for two reasons. First, it assumes that those in minimum security prisons, including many white-collar criminals, are not "real criminals" when in fact they are as "real as they come." Second, it assumes that the incarceration experience in minimum security prisons is not a punitive experience for white-collar offenders. Many white-collar offenders who have been incarcerated, regardless of the type of institution, are quick to describe their experience as punitive. Here are a few comments made by incarcerated white-collar offenders to journalists that illustrate this point:

- Any time your freedom and liberty are restricted, you're being punished. There is no question. It's confinement, incarceration, call it what you want. It's not what everyone else has.

- People have to realize that we are in prison. We are being punished. I would never do a crime again.

- There are no good prisons just like there are no good funeral homes.

Prison is a greater lifestyle change for white-collar criminals than for other criminals. Recall that conventional offenders are more likely to have been previously incarcerated. . . . For most white-collar offenders, prison is a "unique experience". Those who have had a great deal of exposure to prison have been found to prefer prison sentences over alternative sanctions such as intensive probation. Without this previous exposure, white-collar offenders are seen as having a greater sensitivity to incarceration. An incarcerated white-collar offender explained, "You're dropped into the middle of a society whose rules and customs you don't understand". Because of their lack of incarceration experience, many white-collar offenders "reject the inmate culture". As an example, one white-collar offender told [a journalist], "I couldn't even adjust to the language. Everybody swore. It was vile and filthy. I was horrified by the whole experience." . . .

The Myth of Never Doing Time

Many individuals believe that white-collar criminals never go to prison. Some contend that powerful offenders are protected in a biased justice system. In addition, the fact that victims are sometimes unwilling to cooperate with justice officials means that some offenders escape prison sentences by escaping prosecution. On a related line, many white-collar crime victims simply want their money back and realize that they will not get their money back as quickly, if at all, if the offender is incarcerated. Despite these beliefs about the use of prison and jail sanctions to punish offenders, recent evidence shows two interesting trends: 1) more white-collar offenders are being sent to prison and 2) certain factors have been shown to influence the likelihood of incarceration of white-collar offenders.

In 1970, only eight percent of cases prosecuted by the federal government were white-collar crime cases. By the 1980s, nearly one in four federal criminal prosecutions were white-collar crime prosecutions, and research showed that white-collar offenders' likelihood of going to prison increased between the 1970s and 1980s. Today, one of two white-collar offenders convicted at the federal level will be incarcerated. Estimates from the 1980s suggest that anywhere from ten to 40 percent of the residents in federal minimum security prisons were white-collar offenders. With this increase in the number of white-collar offenders being sent to jail or prison, white-collar offenders represent a significant proportion of federal inmates.

Though not to the same degree, the number of white-collar offenders prosecuted and sentenced to jail or prison in various states has also increased. For instance, of 41,000 fraud cases in U.S. state courts in 1996, 38 percent of the offenders received a jail or prison sentence. A study by the Insurance Fraud Bureau of Massachusetts of 476 cases of insurance fraud referred to the criminal justice system found the following:

- About 87 percent of the offenders were found guilty and 99 percent of those found guilty received criminal penalties.

- Approximately 44 percent were given jail sentences, and 33 percent were ordered to serve the sentence.

- Sixty percent were given probation or restitution.

- Seventy percent received multiple sentences.

In addition to increases in the number of white-collar offenders being sentenced to prison, there is also evidence that the average prison length for some white-collar offenders has increased. As an illustration, the average prison sentence of criminal cases referred from the Securities and Exchange Commission (SEC) to the U.S. Attorney's Office increased from ten months in 1992 to 49 months in 1998. When all federal prison sentences are considered, average sentence lengths increased from 39 months in 1986 to 54 months in 1997.

Indeed, a considerable number of white-collar offenders are receiving prison sentences at the state and federal levels. Two interesting developments have occurred in the occupational arena as a result of these increases. First, because there are now so many white-collar offenders being sent to jail or prison; former white-collar offenders who spent time incarcerated are presently making a living consulting future white-collar inmates about what to expect in their prison stay. Reportedly, David Novak, who spent time in federal prison for insurance fraud, makes over a $100,000 a year sharing his experiences with future white-collar inmates. Second, in response to the threat of white-collar employees being sent to jail or prison, some companies have developed policies to follow in case one of their executives receives a jail or prison sentence. These policies focus on maintaining effective public relations so that irrational decisions are not made under pressure. The policies focus on efficient fact gathering and the development of strategies to divert attention away from the company in which the offender was employed.

Factors Determining Incarceration

When white-collar offenses are compared with one another (as opposed to comparing them to street offenses), recent research has shown that three factors play a role in determining whether the offender is incarcerated for his or her misdeeds: harm, blameworthiness, and location. Harm is concerned with the actual losses experienced by victims. More harm means a longer sentence. Judges may even go above sentencing guidelines if harm is quite demonstrable. For instance, one offender who was convicted of swindling investors in the amount of $700 million was given a 30-year prison sentence, which represented a ten-year departure from the maximum sentence recommended in the sentencing guidelines.

Blameworthiness refers to the degree to which the offender can actually be blamed for the offenses. In many white-collar offenses, crime occurs not because of the individual, but because of the expectations placed on individuals in those positions. Basically, employees could leave their jobs, but crime may still be found in those same positions. The practice in the early 1990s of a large retail store paying its automotive repair salespersons by commission is an illustration. Many salespeople went out of their way to add on services so they could make more money. The court ruled that these actions were wrong, although they occurred because of expectations the or-

175

Experiences of White-Collar Inmates

Source	How White-Collar Offenders Experience This
Loss of status	Referred to as a fall from grace, the white-collar inmates status changes more than conventional inmates because they fall further down the "social class ladder."
Lack of privacy	White-collar inmates, like other inmates, have virtually no privacy. Unlike conventional inmates, they have fewer peers with whom they can identify while they are incarcerated.
Identity loss	Many white-collar inmates will lose their sense of self when they are incarcerated. Because they served time, white-collar inmates will be labeled negatively by members of society. In their peer group criminal justice involvement is seen as a blight on one's character. For many conventional criminals, criminal justice involvement is seen as a sign of status among their peers.
Loss of freedom	Like conventional inmates, white-collar offenders lose their freedom. The loss of freedom experienced by white-collar inmates, particularly those who had no previous involvement with the justice system, was more unexpected and potentially more difficult to accept.
Loss of future	Because they committed crimes related to their career, their future as they once imagined it ceased to exist. Most will never again be able to work in their original career.

Brian K. Payne,
Incarcerating White-Collar Offenders, *2003.*

ganization placed on its employees. The retail store was forced to quit paying its automotive salespeople by commission.

Another factor that seems to influence whether a white-collar offender goes to prison is a factor that also determines property value—location, location, location. In particular, recent research cited by [journalist Michael] Higgins (1999) suggests that whether a white-collar defendant ends up in prison depends on where the case is heard. Transaction Records Access Clearinghouse, a group composed of researchers affiliated with Syracuse University, analyzed data supplied by the Department of Justice. Among other things, the researchers found:

- One in two white-collar offenders convicted in federal court was sent to prison.

- In the western district of Wisconsin, eight of ten white-collar crime convictions resulted in a prison sentence.

- In a district of New Jersey, three of ten white-collar crime convictions resulted in a prison sentence.

Attorneys point out that the role of location may not be as important as is demonstrated by these findings. Certain districts might use different practices to target white-collar offenses. A sting operation in one district could result in an increase in convictions making it seem that the district is more punitive than other districts when in fact actual punitiveness is the same. Or, rural districts may hear less serious cases decreasing the likelihood of prison. Others point out that the definition of white-collar crime used by the Syracuse researchers is not clear, and statistics could be manipulated to show just about anything. Regardless of whether there is disparity between districts, one must ask why there has been an overall increase in the number of white-collar offenders sentenced to jail or prison.

Why More Are Being Jailed

Thus far, attention has been paid to specific myths about white-collar crime and the increase in the number of white-collar offenders in prisons and jails. To fully understand the plight of incarcerated white-collar offenders, attention must be given to potential reasons why more white-collar offenders are being sent to jail and prison. . . .

One possible reason for the increase in the number of white-collar inmates is that there are more white-collar offenses being committed. With technological advances and broader political changes, some have argued that crimes such as computer crime, medical fraud, credit card fraud, and telemarketing fraud have been on the rise. If more offenses are occurring, one would expect more arrests, prosecutions, and convictions of white-collar offenders. Indeed, arrests for fraud and embezzlement went up 25 percent and 56 percent respectively between 1983 and 1992.

Another possible reason for the increase in the number of white-collar inmates is that different agencies have increased their investigation and prosecution efforts. To increase certain types of white-collar crime investigation in the late 1980s and early 1990s, President George H.W. Bush announced that an extra $50 million would be provided to investigatory agencies so that the number of officials investigating fraud would double. Around the same time, sophisticated investigative tools typically reserved for street crimes (e.g., search warrants, electronic surveillance, forfeiture proceedings, and undercover investigations) were increasingly used against white-collar offenders. The result has been that, in recent times, some types of white-collar offenses have higher clearance rates than many street crimes. For instance, data from Canada suggests that credit card fraud is four times more likely to be cleared than breaking and entering is. Today, white-collar crime has been cited as the FBI's "largest criminal investigation program, with more than 2,600 pending cases".

Because more cases were being investigated, prosecutors also increased their efforts in combating white-collar crime. Criminal prosecutors became better trained on how to aggressively prosecute offenders, and special prosecutor's offices were created to battle certain kinds of white-collar offenses in various jurisdictions across the United States and Canada. In addition, in many states and at the federal level, the discretion typically afforded to judges in white-collar crime cases was taken away from judges, who are often viewed as lenient toward white-collar offenders, and given to prosecutors, who are seen as more punitive.

Changes in sentencing policies also potentially played a role in increasing the number of incarcerated white-collar offenders. Many states increased their penalties for different white-collar offenses. At the federal level, the U.S. Sentencing Commission's Sentencing Guidelines, developed in 1987, controlled judicial discretion by providing a "cookbook" for determining sanctions given to white-collar offenders. These guidelines made "jail more likely for white-collar offenders" and "sharply increased sentences for white-collar crimes".

Another potential reason that more white-collar offenders began to be sentenced to jail or prison is that the public grew increasingly less tolerant of these offenses in the 1980s. A strong victim's rights movement called for tougher responses toward white-collar offenders. Many prosecutors, judges, and political officials likely wanted to display that they too had a strong disdain for these sorts of misdeeds. Many judges and prosecutors, like politicians, want members of the public to see them as "hard on crime." Accordingly, it is plausible that sentences increased to satisfy the public's desire for retribution.

| "The truth is, we rarely send white-
collar offenders to serve hard time."

White-Collar Criminals Rarely Do Hard Prison Time

David Feige

While the number of white-collar crimes is on the rise and increasingly in the headlines, the accounts of affluent offenders doing prison time are few and far between. David Feige, the author of the following viewpoint, contends that white-collar criminals buck the system because they often have access to the most expensive legal counsel well beyond the means of the middle class. Feige argues that the prospect of not just incarceration but of hard prison time in federal penitentiaries would likely prove a highly effective deterrent in addition to being more just.

David Feige is a former public defender and the author of a book on his experiences, Indefensible: One Lawyer's Journey into the Inferno of American Justice. *He is also the creator and producer of the television series* Raising the Bar *on the TNT network.*

As you read, consider the following questions:

1. According to the author, what are the two "philosophical pillars" of most criminal sentencing schemes?

David Feige, "How To Deter White-Collar Crime," *The Nation*, June 23, 2005. Reproduced by permission.

2. Why in Feige's view is the penal system ineffective for most of the indigent inmates who make up the majority of the prison population?

3. In the author's opinion, why are white-collar criminals likelier "to get away with their crimes than poor folks"?

I t's sweeps week for corporate crooks.

On Monday [June 20, 2005,] US District Judge Leonard Sand sentenced John Rigas, the ailing octogenarian founder and former CEO of Adelphia Communications, to fifteen years in federal prison. Rigas was convicted of fraud and conspiracy charges relating to $50 million in cash advances and $252 million more in margin loans. He has suffered from bladder cancer and underwent triple bypass surgery several years ago.

Rigas's sentence should be of some concern to L. Dennis Kozlowski, the former CEO of Tyco, and Mark Swartz, his main lieutenant. Both of them were convicted by a Manhattan jury just three days earlier on charges relating to the theft of $150 million and the covert sale of stock worth nearly $500 million more. The Tyco convictions (twenty-two counts each) cap a three-year investigation involving two trials, nearly ten months of testimony and several weeks of jury deliberations. . . .

But as huge as a half-billion-dollar fraud may be, both the Adelphia and Tyco cases pale in comparison to the verdict returned on March 15 [2005] against former WorldCom CEO Bernard Ebbers, who was convicted of engineering an unprecedented $11 billion fraud. . . .

Because the Supreme Court has declared the federal sentencing guidelines to be advisory rather than mandatory, US District Judge Barbara Jones (like Judge Sand before her) will have extraordinary latitude when she sentences Ebbers. Technically free to impose a sentence she deems just in light of all the facts and circumstances, Judge Jones could, in theory, order anything from home confinement to a functional life sentence (Ebbers is 63). And she is not alone. Even in state court, where Kozlowski and Swartz will meet their fate, Judge Michael Obus has the discretion to impose a sentence that could wind up being as short as a year or as long as two decades.

Location More than Length

Both judges are allowed to do something else, too: each may make a nonbinding recommendation about where the defendants should serve their respective sentences. (The Bureau of Prisons makes the final decision.) And though the headlines are certain to focus on the number of years each judge imposes, it is actually this recommendation, rather than the length of the sentence, that may be the most effective way for a judge to deter corporate crime.

Most sentencing schemes rest on two philosophical pillars—the idea of just deserts and the notion that penal sanction decreases the likelihood of future crime, either through the incapacitation of the offender or by deterring others. And while just deserts are often invoked in the stern lectures of judges sentencing individual offenders, it is the power of deterrence that is regularly cited by politicians around the country to justify ever-harsher criminal laws and ever more draconian sentencing measures. Standing before the cameras, our lawmakers insistently talk of insuring that bad guys will "think twice" before committing whatever act they happen to be railing against.

But will they?

Rational Criminals

Deterrence is a funny thing. In a 2001 paper that surveyed the research on the deterrent effect of the death penalty, the Maryland State Commission on Criminal Sentencing Policy concluded that the death penalty does not have a deterrent effect. Similar studies in different contexts have come to the same conclusion. To many people who have spent time in the system, these findings make sense—after all, the idea of deterrence rests on the assumption that criminal defendants are rational actors dispassionately assessing criminality as a life choice.

In fact, though, very few of those processed by the criminal justice system are actually rational actors—instead, most are driven by impulses far more powerful than reason. To a crack addict, the only question is whether a robbery will net the $5 necessary for another hit. Two years or 200 is utterly beside the point. For most of the indigent involved in the criminal justice system, crime—whether robbing someone to get high, beating or shooting someone in a fight or fit of rage, or stealing out of hunger—is about addiction, fury, fear, hunger or need. They don't stop to wonder about punishment, and no amount of penal law posturing will stay their hands.

Ebbers, Kozlowski and Rigas, on the other hand, represent something we rarely see in the criminal justice system: true rational actors.

Ebbers and his ilk are intimately acquainted with the nuances of criminal law, the boundaries of accounting fraud and the implications of measures like the Sarbanes-Oxley Act, which is designed to make them more accountable. Moreover, they have access to expensive accountants and advisers well versed in the enforcement practices of the regulators who oversee their industries. Men like Ebbers (or Ken Lay or Jeff Skilling . . . in the Enron debacle) weigh their options—objectively assessing risk and reward. This may make them canny crooks, but it also makes them supremely responsive to the deterrent factors that most legal economists wrongly imagine apply to everyone—chief among them is fear.

Traditionally, there is not a lot of fear in the tony precincts where white-collar criminals dwell. The truth is, we rarely send white-collar offenders to serve hard time. Because of their wealth, privilege and relative sophistication, white-collar criminals can count on gaining significant advantages at every stage of a criminal justice proceeding.

Sending a Message

Because of spotty enforcement, white-collar criminals are far more likely to get away with their crimes than poor folks. And when they are caught, wealthy corporate executives can take refuge in their powerful friends and associates while availing themselves of high-priced lawyers, jury-selection experts and mitigation specialists. The truth is, most corporate crooks get the best representation money can buy, and money, in the criminal justice system, can buy quite a bit. Unlike average criminal defendants, who have few reasonable expectations about where they will do their time, white-collar criminals usually employ consultants to help insure that the defendants serve their sentences under conditions of confinement that, while never pleasant, are nonetheless tolerable. And it works. Because so much of corporate crime is adjudicated in federal rather than state court, corporate criminals often serve their time under relatively cushy conditions of confinement.

Indeed, a slew of high-profile defendants, from Alfred Taubman to Martha Stewart, have recently emerged from their sentences trim, posh and still profitable. And though extended confinement like that initially imposed on junk-bond king Michael Milken may be something of a deterrent, relative rarity and palatable conditions of confinement severely limit the deterrent effect on those considering multimillion-dollar schemes that run afoul of the law. Put bluntly, it's not irrational to steal $10 million if the worst-case scenario is a few years in Camp Fed. But change that sentence to read Sing Sing or Attica or Pelican Bay and what emerges is a whole new calculus of crime.

In dealing with rational actors, it may well be that the conditions of confinement matter far more than the length of the sentence.

White-collar crimes are about greed and self-aggrandizement, and while those things may be deeply compelling, they are fundamentally different from hunger, addiction or desperation. Unlike them, greed responds to fear, and fear is more about the conditions of confinement than its duration. The truth is that to most people, the prospect of even a short stint in a maximum-security prison is far more frightening than years in Camp Fed.

So if during the upcoming parade of CEO sentencing Judge Jones wants to "send a message" in order to deter corporate crime, maybe she should suggest that the Bureau of Prisons save a cell in Leavenworth for Ebbers and his ilk.

> "A system has evolved in the United
> States that . . . subjects [white-collar]
> offenders to draconian sentences that in
> some cases exceed their life expectancy."

Laws Against White-Collar Crime Are Overly Harsh

Ellen S. Podgor

Few people sympathize with white-collar criminals, argues Ellen S. Podgor, the author of the following viewpoint, which in itself condemns them to unfair treatment in criminal sentencing. Despite the statistics Podgor cites indicating that most white-collar criminals are nonviolent first-time offenders, she claims that the majority are issued prison sentences far harsher than even those given to people who commit homicides.

Ellen S. Podgor is an associate professor of law at Stetson University College of Law and coauthor of the book Mastering Criminal Law.

As you read, consider the following questions:

1. What are two discrepancies the author describes in the way the Department of Justice recognizes white-collar crime?

Ellen S. Podgor, "The Challenge of White Collar Sentencing," *Journal of Criminal Law and Criminology*, vol. 97, Spring 2007, pp. 731–759. Copyright © 2007 by Northwestern University, School of Law. Reproduced by permission.

2. In Podgor's view, what type of collateral consequences are white-collar offenders often subject to?

3. What is one of the factors the author claims is often overlooked when officials are administrating federal sentencing?

White collar offenders in the United States have faced sentences far beyond those imposed in prior years. For example, Bernard Ebbers, former CEO of WorldCom, was sentenced to twenty-five years; Jeffrey Skilling, former CEO of Enron, was sentenced to twenty-four years and four months; and Adelphia founder John Rigas received a sentence of fifteen years, with his son Timothy Rigas, the CFO of the company, receiving a twenty-year sentence.

These greatly increased sentences result in part from the employment of the United States sentencing guidelines structure, which includes in the computation of time the amount of fraud loss suffered. Although the sentencing guidelines have some flexibility resulting from the [2005] Supreme Court decision in *United States v. Booker*, the culture of mandated guidelines still permeates the structure and, as such, prominently advises the judiciary. Equally influential in these sentences is the fact that because parole no longer exists in the federal system, the time given to these individuals will likely be in close proximity to the sentence that they will serve.

Although many are quick to denounce the conduct of these individuals and desire lengthy retributive sentences, their disgust with this criminality often overlooks a commonality among these white collar offenders. Each of these individuals has no history of prior criminal conduct. The corporate white collar offenders of today are typically individuals who have never been convicted of criminal conduct and are now facing incredibly long sentences as first offenders. The sentences imposed on these first offenders for economic crimes can exceed the sentences seen for violent street crimes, such as murder or rape.

In an effort to crack down on white collar criminality, the courts and legislature have produced draconian sentences that place prominence on the activity involved, in contrast to the approach taken with recidivist statutes such as "three strikes" laws, the focus in white collar sentencing is on the offense, with little recognition given to the clean slate of these offenders. . . .

White collar sentences need to be reevaluated. In an attempt to achieve a neutral sentencing methodology, one that is class-blind, a system has evolved in the United States that fails to recognize unique qualities of white collar offenders, fails to balance consideration of both the acts and the actors, and subjects these offenders to draconian sentences that in some cases exceed their life expectancy. In essence, the mathematical computations that form the essence of sentencing in the federal system fail to recognize the sociological roots of white collar crime.

Department of Justice Approach

White collar crime is a relatively new concept. Yet despite its recent vintage, it has not been consistently approached by all constituencies. Initially a sociological concept, "white collar crime" is recognized today as a legal term. Translating the sociological concept into a legal one presents deficiencies when placed in the context of the federal sentencing guidelines structure. . . .

White collar crime definitions often recognize the economic nature of this type of crime. Key components tend to be "deception and absence of physical force." But when examining a criminal statute such as the Racketeer Influenced and Corrupt Organizations Act (RICO), determining whether the offense fits the white collar crime category may be dependent on the specific conduct involved. If the conduct is fraud and the predicate act is mail or wire fraud, it should be designated as a white collar crime. When, however, the RICO predicate relates to a state-based offense such as murder or robbery, it should clearly be outside the realm of being a white collar crime. As such, looking at the specific statute in the abstract may not determine whether the activity should be called a white collar crime. The circumstances of the conduct may be equally important in categorizing the activity.

One finds a noticeable discrepancy in the way the Department of Justice (DOJ) recognizes white collar crime. First, in DOJ literature, there is no explicit category called "white collar crime," yet there is continual usage of this term. Second, the Trac Reporting System of the DOJ includes antitrust and fraud as white collar crime but fails to include corruption as well as a host of other criminal activity that most people would consider as belonging to this category. The DOJ also does not include environmental offenses, bribery, federal corruption, procurement corruption, state and local corruption, immigration violations, money laundering, OSHA [Occupational Safety and Health Administration] violations, or copyright violations as white collar crime. Each of these forms of criminal conduct is reported in separate categories exclusive of white collar crime. Thus, when the Trac Reporting System finds a "decline of about ten percent from FY [fiscal year] 2003 to FY 2004" in white collar crime, the omission of many categories raises doubts about the accuracy of the reporting methodology.

Even subdivisions of the DOJ do not concur with the existing reporting system. For example, the United States Attorney's Office for the Northern District of California includes public corruption within its prosecutions of white collar crime. This same office also includes environmental offenses, as well as crimes concerning the Food and Drug Administration as white collar crime, and reports on their white collar prosecutions explicitly using this designation. . . .

The Perils of Wealth

The defendants in corporate fraud accounting cases are basically law-abiding citizens who have not had criminal problems in the past. For example, both Bernard Ebbers and Jeffrey Skilling were first offenders. If defendants who commit corporate frauds had been caught early in their schemes, the damages might not have been as significant as represented in so many of these cases. The crimes committed by those in the corporate world often present larger social harms because of the great number of victims and the enormous economic loss to these victims. Clearly, many individuals lost pension funds and life savings as a result of these wrongdoings. Likewise, it is evident that sharp punishment is in order to deter this criminal conduct.

Defendants charged with corporate frauds seldom require a court-appointed attorney as their wealth places them in an above-average socioeconomic level. Yet because they are at the top, they have farther to fall.

In addition to the powerful position that these individuals may hold, white collar offenders can often be subject to collateral consequences. If lawyers, they are likely to lose their ability to practice law. If stockbrokers, it is unlikely that they will be able to return to their profession. And if part of the medical field, the government may exclude them from federal programs. Unlike the plumber or gardener, a white collar offender is often unable to return to his or her livelihood after serving imprisonment. Licensing, debarment, and government exclusion from benefits may preclude these professionals from resuming the livelihoods held before their convictions. White collar offenders often receive a higher sentence for having a skill, and they can suffer additionally by the collateral consequences that accompany that skill.

Re-entry into society can also be problematic for the white collar offender. While some criminal defendants may think of criminal charges as "catching a case," and, as such, acceptable in society, the white collar offender's country club society is often gone when the person completes his or her sentence. Also, because of the power and prestige held by the corporate-related offender, the person is more likely to feel a greater shame in the community. Being a "front-pager" can subject the individual to more scrutiny and negative publicity, something that might not be felt by individuals of lesser status in society.

Clearly these factors are not persuasive to the general public, as wealth, education, and prestige are often cited as reasons for giving white collar offenders a harsher punishment. The lack of sympathy from the general public makes white collar offenders easy targets for increased punishment.

The Offender's Culpability

There are a wide range of different offenders, each demonstrating different levels of culpability. One finds the mid- to upper-level executive who is heavily involved in the criminal conduct but does not hold the position of CEO. Then there is the CEO who may not be the one who devises the scheme but tolerates or promotes it by his or her high level in the company. There is also the mid- to lower-level individual who participates in the conduct for personal gain or promotion within the company but is not the key player in devising the corporate scheme. Finally, some white collar offenders commit their acts because they want to impress their superiors by showing inflated company profits. This last type of individual may not actually be receiving a personal benefit beyond company recognition. . . .

When a CEO or high-level executive stumbles onto fraudulent activity, discovering the fraud places the CEO in the difficult position of protecting the company while not perpetuating the activity. The court in *United States v. Adelson* described the former Chief Operating Officer and President of Impath, Inc., a company involved in cancer diagnosis testing, as having

Prison Time Gets Harder

John Rusnak's ethics were bad. His timing was considerably worse. Rusnak, 39, a currency trader, pleaded guilty [in 2002] to altering the books at the Baltimore branch of Allfirst bank to hide $700 million in bad trades that won him hefty bonuses.

The first prominent white-collar offender sentenced after Enron, WorldCom and a host of other business giants imploded in scandal, Rusnak ran into a Justice Department unwilling to guarantee that executive felons like him would do easy time in "Club Fed"-style prison camps. Now, more will do much longer sentences in tougher prisons. . . .

Among those Rusnak joined in the federal prison here, which is classified as low security: New Jersey penny-stock promoter Robert Brennan, convicted of bankruptcy fraud and money laundering; former Providence mayor Vincent "Buddy" Cianci Jr., convicted of racketeering conspiracy; and 4,500 less-prominent offenders, many of them drug or immigration law violators. . . .

Jayne O'Donnell and Richard Willing,
USA Today, *May 11, 2003.*

been "sucked into the fraud not because he sought to inflate the company's earnings, but because, as President of the company, he feared the effects of exposing what he had belatedly learned was the substantial fraud perpetrated by others." Judge Rakoff, the district court judge authoring the opinion in this case, took the bold step of moving away from the mathematics of the sentencing guidelines to factor in all aspects of offender culpability. The government, however, has filed a notice of appeal in this case.

The convicted defendants in all these cases were clearly speeding down the corporate highway. The fact that others might speed is irrelevant. The fact that there is no intent to hurt someone is also unimportant. The overriding fact is that they engaged in illegalities and a wreck occurred. If the sentencing guidelines are strictly adhered to, the consequences of the wreck determine the sentence imposed. . . .

Those caught in the initial net thrown into the sea of criminal conduct are likely to be offenders who understood their conduct might not be proper but did not realize it could produce criminal charges and draconian sentences. Although the statutes used, such as mail or wire fraud, may have been on the books for many years, the statutes' application to this form of criminality may be new. . . .

Unfair Sentencing Factors

The individual's motive in committing the crime may also be overlooked in the federal sentencing process. Although motive has never been a mandate of intent and may not be a factor in determining guilt or innocence, motive can be a consideration in punishment theory. The federal sentencing guidelines, however, do not for the most part examine the accused's motive, and only creative post-Booker courts have chanced going down this avenue. As such, the accused that causes an astronomical loss to the public but gains no individual profit may be treated in a similar manner to the individual who might be purchasing costly shower curtains for his home from the profits of his or her corporate fraud. Circuit Judge [Terence] Evans, found in *United States v. Corry* that motive to the victim is "mostly irrelevant" and therefore not something to consider in sentencing. He stated, "[i]f someone steals your wallet and gives the money in it to the Humane Society, rather than blowing it in Las Vegas, that's little comfort as you gaze at your empty pocket." . . .

In addition to the loss factor being a crucial component in determining a sentence, the extent that a person will be punished is also contingent on whether the individual risks a trial. Those who go to trial and are not acquitted face incredibly high sentences. In contrast, those who work with the government and accept a plea with cooperation can reduce their sentences substantially. One need only look at the disparity in sentences between Jeffrey Skilling's sentence of twenty-four years and four months following a trial and [fellow Enron accused] Andrew Fastow's six-year sentence following a plea and cooperation with the government. As such, in making the decision to proceed to trial, individuals who believe themselves innocent face enormous sentencing risks should the jury think otherwise. Although courts are instructed to "avoid the unwarranted sentence disparities among defendants with similar records who have been found guilty of similar conduct," cooperation can serve as a "reasonable explanation" for a noticeable sentencing differential. . . .

Individuals taking the risk of going to trial are not usually schooled in the realities of the criminal process and the prison system, as they are first offenders. Deciding whether to take the risk may also be a function of money, as the cost of legal counsel can influence the ability to spend the sums necessary for a trial, thus forcing a plea negotiation to preserve assets for the offender's family.

Sentencing in the federal system does not account for the risk taken by the individual who goes to trial. In fact, it works against this person by having him or her receive a higher sentence than could have been obtained if the defendant had not demanded enforcement of the constitutional right to a jury trial.

An additional factor that compounds this risk is the recent flux of deferred prosecution agreements. These agreements provide the corporation with a benefit, often to the detriment of the individual. The government leverages the corporation against the individual, demanding total cooperation in its investigation. Corporations agreeing to deferred prosecution agreements can sometimes become mini-prosecutors in an effort to appease the government. . . .

A Strict Quantitative Approach

The one-size-fits-all methodology of sentencing white collar offenders seriously diminishes consideration of the individual offender, the nature of the offense, and the level of protection needed to satisfy the public's interest. It provides a mathematical computation for determining the sentence without regard to sociological differences.

1. Failure to Consider the Offender

The federal sentencing guidelines fail to adequately examine the individual offender in determining the sentence. Omitted from consideration are the collateral consequences faced by the offender and the differences he or she faces upon reentry into society. The specific culpability of the individual also is not considered. Courts do not focus on whether the accused had the benefit of seeing prior individuals receive harsh penalties and thus was able to have the benefit of deterrence prior to their committing the act, or, alternatively, whether the accused was caught committing the crime du jour without realizing that the activity is not acceptable business conduct.

Culpability is basically non-existent as a sentencing concern, with the punishment resting on a numerical figure that correlates with the amount of loss occurring as a result of the crime. Courts seldom consider where the individual may be on the corporate ladder, the extent to which he or she is directly engaged in the criminal conduct, and any individual profit obtained as a result of engaging in the improper activity. In essence, sentencing fails to account for a difference between the CEO heavily entrenched in the criminal behavior and the CEO with little knowledge of criminal wrongdoing.

Also omitted from the review process is the motivation of the accused and the actual benefit received by this individual.

2. Failure to Consider the Uniqueness of White Collar Crimes

The failure to focus on the offender is exacerbated by the fact that the crimes used in white collar cases have little or no flexibility. Unlike many state offenses, there are no degrees or lesser included offenses to these crimes. For example, a homicide can be many different crimes dependent upon factors such as heat of passion, deliberation, premeditation, cooling off period, or extreme emotional disturbance. Irrespective of the jurisdiction or the grading methodology used, the offense level is adjusted by the culpability of the accused. An unlawful killing can range from being considered murder in the first degree, voluntary manslaughter, or reckless homicide, to perhaps a vehicular homicide, depending on the specific laws of the jurisdiction.

One does not find these lesser included offenses with white collar crimes as there are no degrees or levels of punishment. The classic white collar crimes—bank fraud, mail fraud, and wire fraud—are not predicated on lower level crimes with a lesser degree of culpability or extenuating circumstances. The individual is either guilty or not guilty of the designated offense.

3. Future Dangerousness

Perhaps the most noticeable characteristic omitted by the quantitative approach to sentencing is future dangerousness. White collar offenders, especially those coming from the corporate arena, are usually first offenders. Additionally, there is little likelihood of recidivism. The individual seldom can resume a position of power that would allow for continued criminality of this nature.

The court also has the ability to limit any future dangerousness by precluding the individual from serving in a future corporate position. For example, in his sentencing of Richard

P. Adelson, former Chief Operating Office and President of Impath, the Honorable Jed Rakoff stated that "[w]ith [Adelson's] reputation ruined by his conviction, it was extremely unlikely that he would ever involve himself in future misconduct. Just to be sure, however, the Court, as part of the sentence here imposed, barred Adelson from ever again serving as an officer or director of a public company."

If sentencing has as a goal the protection of society, factoring in the future dangerousness of the individual is an important component of the system. With the elimination of the individual's corporate role, the stripping of the convicted felon's money, and the accompanying collateral consequences, such as a loss of license or ability to conduct business with the government, future dangerousness is nearly eliminated.

Punishment Theory

All of criminal law revolves around punishment theory. We create laws in order to punish conduct that society finds abhorrent. We then enforce these laws and punish offenders in order to secure adherence to the laws. The classic theories consider utilitarian models that encompass goals of deterrence, both general and specific, rehabilitation, isolation, and education. On the other hand, there is retributive theory that punishes for the sake of "paying the debt to society." Punishment theory is also multidimensional, with considerations of communicative retribution looking at not only the specific wrongs to victims but also the repercussions to society and groups within society that might suffer as a result of the wrongful act.

Sentencing of offenders is the last stage of punishment theory. It is the one portion of the criminal process when the court can examine individual culpability in relation to the offense committed. De-emphasizing this consideration because of concerns that class may play a factor in the sentence works to eliminate considerations unique to many corporate white collar offenders.

Sentencing needs to remain fluid to account for all considerations and yet also be transparent for review. Most importantly, we need to infuse into the sentencing process some of the sociological teachings that started the discussion of white collar crime. It is important to strive for a sentencing system that is classless, but in doing so it is also important to respect real differences.

> *"As businesses and financial transactions become more and more computer and Internet dependent, the reality of increased economic crime grows exponentially, fueled by the rapid growth of technology."*

White-Collar Crime Laws Need Toughening in Response to New Technologies

Richard Johnston

Although most criminologists concur that white-collar crime is more pervasive, serious, and costly than any other type, it is also among the most difficult to combat. A chief reason for this, according to Richard Johnston, the author of the following viewpoint, is the sheer complexity of the modern Internet age. Johnston notes that the expansiveness and fluid nature of globalized e-commerce make it unusually challenging to compile reliable statistics on cybercrimes, let alone to track down perpetrators. Johnston also claims that government resources allocated to deal with online crimes is comparatively minimal, even though such crimes are steeply on the rise compared to violent crimes.

Richard Johnston, "The Battle Against White-Collar Crime," *USA Today*, vol. 130, January 2002, pp. 36–38. Copyright © 2002 Society for the Advancement of Education. Reproduced by permission.

Richard Johnston is director of the National White Collar Crime Center in Richmond, Virginia and the author of numerous articles on the subject.

As you read, consider the following questions:

1. How in the author's view has the globalization of Internet communication and commerce significantly affected the manner in which economic crimes are committed?

2. What are some of the challenges Johnston cites that make fighting white-collar crime unusually difficult?

3. According to the author, what were three of the issues for combating cybercrime that were raised at meetings of the National Cybercrime Training Partnership?

One in three American households are victims of white-collar crime, yet just 41% actually report it. Of those reported, a mere 21% made it into the hands of a law enforcement or consumer protection agency. This means that less than eight percent of white-collar crimes reached the proper authorities, according to the National Public Survey on White Collar Crime, a groundbreaking survey conducted by the National White Collar Crime Center (NW3C), a nonprofit, Federally funded organization that supports state and local police in their efforts to prevent, investigate, and prosecute economic and high-tech crime. For consumers and businesses alike, these statistics are unsettling as the threat of white-collar crimes invades our new, high-tech society.

Why do Americans fail to report these crimes that are costing the nation hundreds of billions of dollars every year? Our statistics show that there is a wide disparity between how people believe they will react when they are victimized and how they do so when they actually are. One reason may be that they may not have initially considered the offenses to them as crimes; they may have been uncertain about which agency to contact; or they may have a lack of faith that the offenders would be apprehended.

Technology Fuels White-Collar Crime

White-collar crimes come in many different forms, including money laundering; credit card, health care, insurance, securities, and/or telecommunications fraud; intellectual property and computer crimes; and identity theft. The growth of the information age and the globalization of Internet communication and commerce have impacted significantly upon the manner in which economic crimes are committed, their frequency, and the difficulty in apprehending the perpetrators.

According to the National Fraud Center statistics, economic crime cost the nation $5,000,000,000 in 1970, $20,000,000,000 in 1980, and $100,000,000,000 in 1990. As businesses and financial transactions become more and more computer and Internet dependent, the reality of increased economic crime grows exponentially, fueled by the rapid growth of technology.

The Federal Bureau of Investigation's Uniform Crime Reports national arrest statistics for the period 1988–97 show that, while arrests for most index crimes of violence (e.g., murder, nonnegligent manslaughter, rape) and property crimes (robbery, burglary, motor vehicle theft) have declined, those for fraud and embezzlement have risen significantly.

Considering the amount of government funding allocated to the control of "street crime" there has been relatively little money set aside for dealing with white-collar crime. This is due in part to a long-standing belief that the public is apathetic towards white-collar offenses and offenders.

The aim of the NW3C in administering the National Public Survey on White Collar Crime was to add broader and more-current information to the insights furnished by prior surveys. Rather than limiting our focus to any one aspect, we touched upon several perception dimensions to present a comprehensive picture of what the average American thinks about white-collar crime. We were interested in obtaining answers to questions such as: How serious do you believe white-collar crime is? How safe do you feel from white-collar crime? Have you or someone in your household been victimized by white-collar crime? If so, did you report the victimization? What type of person do you believe the average white-collar crime victim is? We also asked about participation in risk behaviors associated with white-collar crime victimization, perceptions of the control of white-collar crime; and opinions on workplace theft.

The results proved informative to the law enforcement community, consumer protection organizations, and victim advocacy groups, as well as to criminologists. Statistics to the contrary, the results uncovered a deep concern with white-collar crime and how effectively the criminal justice system deals with such offenses.

Upon assessing the survey results, a multi-layered picture materialized. We found the public is becoming well acquainted with theft by deception (as its victims) and tends to view the commission of such crime with an increasingly jaundiced eye. We were able to conclude that the level of victimization is high when compared to earlier studies. Relying on the survey results alone, it is difficult to explain the underlying reasons for the high incidence of victimization. The FBI's Uniform Crime Reports indicate that arrests for fraud, embezzlement, and forgery have risen nationally over the last several years. The incidence of white-collar crime victimizations culled from our survey may simply be a reflection of a rise in activity in this area. On the other hand, the number of victimizations might be a sign that the people may not be sufficiently aware of their vulnerability to being victimized.

Combating White-Collar Crime

Several channels have contributed to combating economic and high-tech crime:

Independent corporations and private-sector industry coalitions. As a result of limited law enforcement resources, corporations on their own or in cooperation with industry coalitions, such as BITS, the technology group for the Financial Services Roundtable, have had to initiate strategic economic crime-management plans and investigative groups. There is a growing level of frustration among these corporations, because the monetary thresholds for law enforcement even to investigate a case, let alone prosecute, can be very high, depending on the jurisdiction. Coupled with this is increased legislation requiting corporations to institute anti-fraud programs and compliance departments. While protection of corporate assets and their consumers should be their responsibility, there are several consequences to this arrangement. Many economic crimes go unreported; fewer prosecutions of these offenses occur; and perpetrators tend to be fired rather than prosecuted, leaving them free to move on to another organization and continue their victimizing.

Law enforcement. On the Federal level, numerous regulatory and law enforcement agencies are authorized to combat specific economic crimes, including the Federal Bureau of Investigation, Secret Service, Postal Inspection Service, Securities and Exchange Commission, and Customs. Local law enforcement capabilities for combating economic crime vary, depending on the size and location of the department and the allocation of resources. Some larger municipalities and state law enforcement agencies have formed economic and computer crime units. As resources, training, and awareness of the intensity of the problem increase, it is likely and necessary that more of these units will be formed.

National White Collar Crime Center. The NW3C provides programs geared to meet the specific investigative support needs of state and local law enforcement agencies in their fight against economic and high-tech criminal activity. In addition, new projects include the development of the National Fraud Complaint Management Center to leverage technology in the management of economic crime complaints. A significant part of this project is the establishment of the Internet Fraud Complaint Center in partnership with the FBI.

Internet Fraud Complaint Center. The IFCC is a resource established for law enforcement by law enforcement. For victims of Internet fraud, it provides a convenient and easy way to alert authorities of a suspected violation. For law enforcement and regulatory agencies, the IFCC offers a central repository for complaints related to Internet fraud, uses the information to quantify patterns, and provides timely statistical data of current fraud trends. The key to its success lies in its ability to relay timely and complete information to the appropriate local, state, and/or Federal law enforcement agencies. By facilitating the flow of information between law enforcement and victims of fraud, the IFCC streamlines the case initiation effort on behalf of both the victim and law enforcement agencies.

National Cybercrime Training Partnership. Developed by the Department of Justice and managed by the NW3C, the NCTP provides guidance and assistance to local, state, and Federal law enforcement agencies in an effort to ensure that the law enforcement comproperly is properly trained to address electronic and high-technology crime.

Coalition for the Prevention of Economic Crime. A nonprofit organization established in 1996, CPEC provides support services to businesses in their fight against economic crime. Its mission is to raise awareness of such offences and their impact on businesses. CPEC works closely with law enforcement through a partnership with the NW3C. Current training programs include instruction on fraud management; operational and strategic fraud management techniques; financial investigations practical skills, examination, and analysis; basic data recovery and analysis; and instruction on how to use the Internet for investigations and research.

Cyber Insurance

Law enforcement and security officials know it, and so do insurance professionals. In fact, they expect cyber liability to be one of the fastest-growing segments of the national property and casualty market.

So what is cyber insurance? It's a specialized policy that has emerged in recent years in response to cyber crime, also known as computer crime, e-crime and information technology crime.

Who's at risk? You name it—individuals, companies and organizations of all sizes and in every industry.

What does it cover? It's designed to cover potential losses resulting from network security breaches and other [information technology]-related problems. It is considered by industry professionals to be an important risk-management tool.

Dan Kohane, senior partner in the law firm of Hurwitz & Fine P.C., Buffalo, says cyber crime is a big problem that's only going to get bigger.

Jane Schmitt, Bizjournals, *May 28, 2008.*

Needs and Challenges

As a nation, we are faced with an irrefutable challenge to find solutions to the growing threat of white-collar crime. Law enforcement training is key. Preventing, detecting, investigating, and prosecuting economic crimes must become a priority in order to lessen their impact on the economy and the public's confidence. Law enforcement, as it stands now, is in danger of slipping further behind highly sophisticated criminals.

Specialized training in the areas of economic and computer crime, as well as computer forensics, needs to be continued for law enforcement personnel at the Federal, state, and local levels. This is especially important as nearly all white-collar crime now involves computers.

Laws, regulations, and reporting systems are crucial solutions. In the U.S., all levels of government have allowed self-regulation of the Internet. Government regulation, for the most part, has focused on cybercrimes that are not economic ones, such as child pornography and cyberstalking. That attitude appears to be changing. There are numerous bills pending in Congress that address criminal frauds committed on the Internet, identity theft, and issues involving Internet security and attacks upon websites.

Public-private partnerships are essential in this battle. Since no one group will be able to solve the complex problems, coalitions of private and public groups must work together to combat economic and cybercrime. As more of these alliances develop, there will be added resources available to reverse the trend of economic crime. Colleges and universities need to revamp their existing programs to create new ones to meet the changing needs of society in this area.

What makes the solutions a challenge is based on several factors. First, classifying white-collar crimes is difficult. Lack of clear definitions make it hard for categories to be formed and accurate statistics kept. For example, many individuals use the term white-collar crime, financial crime, and computer crime interchangeably, thus complicating the recording methods of each crime.

Another challenge is getting law enforcement and private security professionals to take advantage of the training resources available to them. The reasons this may be occurring include insufficient funding, lack of awareness of the opportunities for training, and a shortage of appropriate staff.

Finally, a big block in the road to solving the white-collar crime threat is the fact that the public perception of fraud and its seriousness has not yet been heightened to an appropriate level of concern. Consumers, businesses, and the nation's lawmakers must be persuaded of the importance in recognizing how high-tech and economic crime affects and impacts on society.

Need for a New Method

The NCTP has conducted several focus group meetings revealing that electronic crime is having a profound effect on law enforcement and that no agency is escaping it. At the meetings, a nationwide survey of 31 state and local law enforcement representatives who impact a training base of more than 84,000 persons concluded that program coordination, fast-track initiatives implementation, and skills training are the keys to fighting this growing concern.

With a purposeful concentration on the state and local police experience, the following issues were raised during the sessions as a needs list for combating cybercrime:

- Public awareness, to educate individuals, elected officials, and businesses about the impact of electronic crime

- Data and reporting, to understand the extent and impact of electronic crime

- Uniform training and certification courses, to train the police to do their jobs

- On-site management assistance for electronic crime units and task forces, to give help in developing properly equipped computer investigation units

- Updated laws applied at the Federal and state levels, in order to keep pace with electronic crime

- Cooperation with the high-tech industry, to control electronic crime and to protect the nation's critical infrastructure

- Special research and publications, to give investigators a comprehensive directory of training and expert resources to aid them in combating electronic crime

- Management awareness and support, to help senior staffers to understand the impact of electronic crime and to support the expertise and tools needed to investigate and prosecute electronic crime cases

- Investigative and forensic tools, to provide the police with up-to-date technology and the tools necessary to conduct electronic crime investigations

- Structuring of a computer crime unit, to establish best practices on how to create a police unit that can investigate and analyze electronic evidence.

Impact of New Initiatives

The NCTP has already begun training programs to address many of these concerns and is giving law enforcement professionals across the nation a place to turn to help consumers with the cybercrime problem. Current initiatives include the development and delivery of electronic and high-technology crime training. The NW3C has developed and deployed computer crime training in the last year alone that has benefited more than 1,400 agencies throughout the U.S. That number continues to grow.

Specialized law enforcement training has had an impact. NCTP training efforts have reached officers on the front lines, forensic specialists, detectives, prosecutors, and others in need of formal relining at either an entry or advanced level, depending on their case involvement.

The Internet Fraud Complaint Center has proven its worth to America's fraud victims, referring large and small complaints to law enforcement agencies nationwide. The IFCC conducted a takedown initiative, code named Operation Cyber Loss, which included efforts by the FBI and numerous state and local police departments. They brought charges against 90 individuals and companies, who face a variety of Federal and state criminal charges, which include fraud by wire, mail fraud, bank fraud, money laundering, and intellectual property rights violations. The schemes exposed as part of this operation represent over 56,000 victims who suffered cumulative losses in excess of $117,000,000.

The IFCC is in a unique position to identify training needs for law enforcement. The NW3C is responding to state and local law enforcement's training requests through its role as Operations Center for the NCTP. The IFCC also continues to expand its capabilities to accommodate the needs of businesses better, as it has begun the work of creating the appropriate channels that will enable regular communication with representatives from private industry across the nation. We continue to invite input from companies to refine the process of how data at the IFCC is collected and quantified.

The exponential growth of technology and the use of computers have triggered a purposeful rethinking of the tools needed by law enforcement organizations to address Internet-related crime. Law enforcement professionals have voiced their concern regarding adequate training in order to be effective in apprehending and prosecuting criminals who use the Internet to facilitate their crimes. State and local police, through their affiliation with the National White Collar Crime Center, have tasked us to help them meet this challenge.

Most individuals are unaware of the extent to which their lives, financial status, businesses, families, or privacy might be affected by electronic crime. Unless individuals, companies, and government officials are informed of the increase in crimes committed using the Internet, cybercriminals will continue to steal people's money, identities, and property.

Periodical Bibliography

Matthew Benjamin   "The Wages of Sin," *U.S. News & World Report*, June 23, 2003.

Daphne Eviatar   "Case Closed?" *Corporate Counsel*, December 2007.

Kathleen Gurley, Paula Wood, and Inder Nijhawan   "The Effect of Punishment on Ethical Behavior When Personal Gain Is Involved," *Journal of Legal, Ethical and Regulatory Issues*, January 2007.

Pamela MacLean   "White-Collar Prosecutions on the Decline," *Connecticut Law Tribune*, December 4, 2006.

Jon May   "Countering Hindsight Bias in White Collar Prosecutions," *Criminal Justice*, Fall 2006.

Wilson Meeks   "Corporate and White-Collar Crime Enforcement: Should Regulation and Rehabilitation Spell an End to Corporate Criminal Liability?" *Columbia Journal of Law and Social Problems*, Fall 2006.

Geraldine Szott Moohr   "What the Martha Stewart Case Tells Us About White Collar Criminal Law," *Houston Law Review*, Summer 2006.

Lisa H. Nicholson   "The Culture of Under-enforcement," *DePaul Business and Commercial Law Journal*, Winter 2007.

Nate Raymond   "No Time to Do Time," *Corporate Counsel*, December 2007.

Andrea Schoepfer, Stephanie Carmichael, and Nicole Leeper Piquero   "Do Perceptions of Punishment Vary Between White-Collar and Street Crimes?" *Journal of Criminal Justice*, March-April 2007.

Irwin M. Stelzer   "Protecting the Innocent: Even White-Collar Defendants Have Rights," *Weekly Standard*, August 21, 2006.

 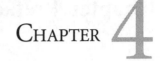

Is White-Collar Crime Institutionalized?

Chapter Preface

In the autumn of 2008, after months of turbulence in the mortgage and credit industries, the American economic system reached an unprecedented state of fragility. The collapse of several major banks within weeks of each other was swiftly followed by the federal takeover of two mortgage corporations that many investors had believed only months previously to be stable and solvent.

Stressing the urgency of the situation, treasury secretary Henry Paulson and Federal Reserve chairman Ben Bernanke introduced the Economic Stabilization Act of 2008, a $700 billion emergency bailout of the U.S. banking system. According to Paulson and Bernanke, the bill was intended to free up credit markets and give banks enough capital to begin lending money again. Although the banks had failed as a combined result of lax regulations by the government, questionable business practices by the companies themselves, and greed or poor foresight on the part of their clients, it was argued by many in the financial district as well as then president George W. Bush that failure to pass the measure immediately might lead to a devastating economic depression.

While public support for the bill was slim and it had already been voted down by the House of Representatives days before, on October 1 the Senate passed an amended version of the program, known as the Troubled Asset Relief Program (TARP), with the first half of the funds to be distributed to eligible financial institutions immediately.

Congressional oversight of the program was considered problematic by many critics from the start. Paulson's original proposal had included a stipulation exempting him from any legal responsibility regarding banks' usage of the funds. Another note of controversy was the fact that some of the banks who received funds had not been among those on the verge of bankruptcy. Adding even further to the growing public outcry, in a December 2008 survey of twenty-one banks that had received TARP funds conducted by the Associated Press in December, not one of the institutions provided specific answers as to how the money had been spent.

Numerous widely corroborated reports circulated that the first half of the funds had not been used to help taxpayers acquire car and home loans as the plan had originally been pitched but rather to help large banks acquire assets, force mergers, and otherwise allow executives to maintain their privileged lifestyle.

Additionally, several members of the Office of Financial Stability panel established to track the usage of the TARP funds, were themselves former bankers and investment magnates, which many critics suggested was a potentially catastrophic, if not criminal, conflict of interest.

Social and financial critics have long complained that while the government is adamant about upholding free market principles when it comes to collecting taxes and outsourcing jobs to other countries, it appears able to simultaneously rack up trillions of dollars in national debt without any administrative oversight and to be quick to provide expensive bailouts to corporations using taxpayer dollars whenever things go sour, even on the occasions when the crisis in question was largely set into motion by the selfsame companies and individuals receiving the funds. Many Wall Street executives, the critics claim, voluntarily leave their positions to pursue political careers in order to help further deregulate the industries that they used to make their own fortunes with the connivance of the last-generation legislators in power ahead of them. The whole American financial system, they argue, is simply an example of how cronyism and corruption have transformed what was once the ideals of democracy into a surprisingly fragile but socially accepted Ponzi scheme directed at the public and smaller businesses.

Defenders of big business counter that enforcing stricter regulations would make it more difficult for American companies to stay competitive in the increasingly globalized marketplace. As online commerce has changed business dynamics, these critics argue, accounting practices based on a traditional paper economy are simply no longer adequate. In their view, corporations need even greater leeway, and they deserve it, they contend, since the rich pay higher taxes and consequently produce more revenue for the government.

Some of the viewpoints collected in this chapter argue that white-collar crime is a necessary evil of any free-market economic system. Other authors contend that economic crimes should not be tolerated at all, let alone be legitimized. Ultimately, while members of both camps disagree on the best solution, all agree that the problem is both deep-rooted and severe.

> *James Madison wrote . . . "[Banks'] advantages, whatever they may be, are outweighed by the excesses of their paper emissions, and the partialities and corruptions with which they are administered."*

The Founding Fathers Considered Corporations Oppressive

Thom Hartmann

Although many people believe that the United States government today is run like a corporation, some, like Thom Hartmann, the author of the following viewpoint, argue that many of the Founding Fathers feared that corporate monopolies, if their power were left unfettered, would eventually undermine the very fabric of democracy. Hartmann notes that many seminal events celebrated by Americans, such as the Boston Tea Party and the American Revolution itself were in fact acts of revolt against the imperialist policies of England not far removed from those espoused by many American corporations today. In Hartmann's view, Thomas Jefferson and James Madison would find the influence and

Thom Hartmann, *Unequal Protection.* Emmaus, PA: Rodale, 2004. © 2002 by Mythical Research, Inc. and Thom Hartmann. Reproduced by permission.

lack of accountability enjoyed by modern media conglomerates nothing short of horrifying and illegal, a complete betrayal of democratic principles.

Thom Hartmann is an author, a nationally syndicated radio talk show host, and holds a PhD in homeopathic medicine.

As you read, consider the following questions:

1. According to the author, why did Federalists like Alexander Hamilton and John Adams object to Thomas Jefferson's notion that a government should be entirely elected and controlled by its people, with minimal taxation and military powers?
2. What did Thomas Jefferson perceive as the three principal threats to human beings' natural rights, as cited by Hartmann?
3. What were Thomas Jefferson's six wishes for the bill of rights, and of them, which two were in the end omitted, according to the author?

Very few people are aware that Thomas Jefferson considered freedom from monopolies to be one of the fundamental human rights. But it was very much a part of his thinking during the time when the Bill of Rights was born.

In fact, most of the founders of America never imagined a huge commercial empire sweeping over their land. . . . Rather, most of them saw an America made up of people like themselves: farmers.

In a speech before Congress on April 9, 1789, James Madison referred to agriculture as the great staple of America. He added, "I think [agriculture] may justly be styled the staple of the United States; from the spontaneous productions which nature furnishes, and the manifest preference it has over every other object of emolument in this country."

In a *National Gazette* article on March 3, 1792, Madison wrote, "The class of citizens who provide at once their own food and their own raiment, may be viewed as the most truly independent and happy. They are more; they are the best basis of public liberty, and the strongest bulwark of public safety. It follows that the greater the proportion of this class to the whole society, the more free, the more independent, and the more happy must be the society itself."

Distrust of Private Corporations

The first large privately owned corporation to rise up in the new United States during the presidential terms of Jefferson (1801 to 1809) and Madison (1809 to 1817) was the Second Bank of the United States. By 1830, the bank was one of the largest and most powerful private corporations, and was even sponsoring its directors and agents as candidates for political office in order to extend its own power.

In President Andrew Jackson's annual message to Congress on December 3, 1833, he explicitly demanded that the bank cease its political activities or receive a corporate death sentence—revocation of its corporate charter. He said, "In this point of the case the question is distinctly presented whether the people of the United States are to govern through representatives chosen by their unbiased suffrages or whether the money and power of a great corporation are to be secretly exerted to influence their judgment and control their decisions."

Jackson succeeded in forcing a withdrawal of all federal funds from the bank that year, putting it out of business. Its federal charter expired in 1836, and was only revived as a state bank authorized by the state of Pennsylvania. It went bankrupt in 1841.

Although thousands of federal, state, county, city, and community laws restrained corporations vastly more than they are today, the presidents who followed Jackson continued to worry out loud about the implications if corporations expanded their power.

In the middle of the 30-year struggle, in May 1827, James Madison wrote a letter to his friend James K. Paulding about the issue. He said, "With regard to Banks, they have taken too deep and too wide a root in social transactions, to be got rid of altogether, if that were desirable. . . . they have a hold on public opinion, which alone would make it expedient to aim rather at the improvement, than the suppression of them. As now generally constituted, their advantages, whatever they be, are outweighed by the excesses of their paper emissions, and the partialities and corruption with which they are administered."

Thus, while Madison saw the rise of corporate power and its dangers during and after his presidency, the issues weren't obvious to him when he was helping write the United States Constitution decades earlier. And that may have been significant when the Bill of Rights was being put together.

Federalists vs. Democratic Republicans

Shortly after George Washington became the first President of the United States in 1789, his Secretary of the Treasury, Alexander Hamilton, proposed that the federal government incorporate a national bank and assume state debts left over from the Revolutionary War. Congressman James Madison and Secretary of State Thomas Jefferson saw this as an inappropriate role for the federal government, representing the potential concentration of too much money and power in the federal government. (The Bill of Rights, with its Tenth Amendment reserving powers to the states, wouldn't be ratified for 2 more years.)

The disagreement over the bank and assuming the states' debt nearly tore apart the new government, and led to the creation by Hamilton, Washington, and Vice President John Adams (among others, including Thomas and Charles Pinckney, Rufus King, DeWitt Clinton, and John Jay) of the Federalist Party.

Several factions arose in opposition to the Federalists, broadly referred to as the Anti-Federalists, including two groups who called themselves Democrats and Republicans. Jefferson pulled them together by 1794 into the Democratic Republican Party, united in their opposition to the Federalists' ideas of a strong central government that could grant the power to incorporate a national bank and bestow benefits to favored businesses through the use of tariffs and trade regulation.

During the Washington and Adams presidencies, however, the Federalists reigned, and Hamilton was successful in pushing through his programs for assuming state debts, creating a United States Bank, and a network of bounties and tariffs to benefit emerging industries and businesses.

In 1794, independent whiskey distillers in Pennsylvania revolted against Hamilton's federal taxes on their product, calling them "unjust, dangerous to liberty, oppressive to the poor, and particularly oppressive to the Western country, where grain could only be disposed of by distilling it."

The whiskey distillers tarred and feathered a tax collector and pulled together a local militia of 7,000 men. But President Washington issued two federal orders and sent in General Henry Lee commanding militias from Pennsylvania, Maryland, New Jersey, and Virginia. To demonstrate his authority as commander-in-chief, Washington rode at the head of the soldiers in their initial attack.

The Whiskey Rebellion was put down and the power of the Federalists wasn't questioned again until the election of 1800, which Jefferson's Democratic Republican party won in an election referred to as the Second American Revolution or the Revolution of 1800.

In the election of 1804, the Federalists carried only Delaware, Connecticut, and part of Maryland against Jefferson's Democratic Republicans (later to become the Democratic Party), and by 1832, as the Industrial Revolution was taking hold of America, the Federalists were so marginalized that they ceased to exist as an organized party.

Jefferson and Natural Rights

Back in the earliest days of the United States, Jefferson didn't anticipate the scope, meaning, and consequences of the Industrial Revolution that was just starting to gather steam in Europe about the time he was entering politics in the Virginia House of Burgesses. He distrusted letting companies have too much power, but he was focusing on the concept of "natural rights," an idea which was at the core of the writings and speeches of most of the Revolutionary-era generation, from Thomas Paine to Patrick Henry to Benjamin Franklin.

In Jefferson's mind, "the natural rights of man" were enjoyed by Jefferson's ancient tribal ancestors of Europe, were lived out during Jefferson's life by some of the tribal peoples of North America, and were written about most explicitly 60 years before Jefferson's birth by John Locke, whose writings were widely known and often referenced in pre-Revolutionary America.

Natural rights, Locke said, are things that people are born with simply by virtue of their being human and born into the world. In 1690, in his "Second Treatise on Government," Locke put forth one of the most well-known definitions of the natural rights that all people are heirs to by virtue of their common humanity. He wrote, "All men by nature are equal . . . in that equal right that every man hath to his natural freedom, without being subjected to the will or authority of any other man . . . being all equal and independent, no one ought to harm another in his life, health, liberty or possessions. . . ."

As to the role of government, Locke wrote, "Men being . . . by nature all free, equal and independent, no one can be put out of his estate and subjected to the political power of another without his own consent which is done by agreeing with other men, to join and unite into a community for their comfortable, safe, and peaceable living . . . in a secure enjoyment of their properties. . . ."

This natural right was asserted by Jefferson first in his "Summary View of the Rights of British America," published in 1774, in which he wrote, "The God who gave us life gave us liberty at the same time; the hand of force may destroy, but cannot disjoin them." His first draft of the Declaration of Independence similarly declared, "We hold these truths to be sacred and undeniable; that all men are created equal and independent, that from that equal creation they derive rights inherent and unalienable, among which are the preservation of life, and liberty, and the pursuit of happiness."

Individuals asserted those natural rights in the form of a representative government that *they controlled*, and that same government also protected their natural rights from all the forces that in previous lands had dominated, enslaved, and taken advantage of them.

Danger of Full Natural Rights

Hamilton and Adams' Federalists, as we can read in *The Federalist Papers*, strongly objected to Jefferson and Madison's notion that a government should be entirely elected and controlled by its people, with minimal taxation and military powers.

They were worried that if there wasn't a strong federal government, with a perpetual army, taxation powers, and at least half the legislature (the Senate) made up of an elite appointed by professional politicians from the states, the newly born United States might be too weak to fend off external foes like the French and Spanish—who both had stakes in North America at that time—or to put down possible future internal rebellions.

They suggested that Jefferson and Madison were idealists and dreamers, trying to recreate a utopian society in a dangerous world. Hamilton wrote about the risks of such idealism, responding to Madison, in *Federalist* No. 30, saying, "Reflections of this kind may have trifling weight with men [like you] who hope to see realized in America the halcyon scenes of the poetic or fabulous age; but to those [among us Federalists] who believe we are likely to experience a common portion of the vicissitudes and calamities which have fallen to the lot of other nations, they must appear entitled to serious attention. Such men [as those of us who would lead this nation] must behold the actual situation of their country with painful solicitude, and depreciate the evils which ambition or revenge might, with too much facility, inflict upon it."

Nonetheless, over the strong objections of the Federalists, James Madison pressed through Congress the Bill of Rights, which he had worked out in correspondence with Jefferson. Made up of the first 10 amendments to the Constitution, the Bill of Rights in its entirety was designed by Madison and Jefferson to prevent government from ever taking for itself the rights that they considered to be natural and God-given.

The Three Threats

Thomas Jefferson's vision of America was quite straightforward. In its simplest form, he saw a society where people were first and institutions were second. In his day, Jefferson saw three agencies that were threats to humans' natural rights. They were:

- Governments (particularly in the form of kingdoms and elite groups like the Federalists)

- Organized religions (he rewrote the New Testament to take out all the "miracles" so that in *The Jefferson Bible* Jesus became a proponent of God-given natural rights)

- Commercial monopolies and the "pseudo aristoi," or pseudo aristocracy (in the form of extremely wealthy individuals and overly powerful corporations)

Instead, he believed it was possible for people to live by self-government in a nation in which nobody controlled the people except the people themselves. He found evidence for this belief both in the cultures of Native Americans such as the Cherokee and the Iroquois Confederation, which he studied extensively; in the political experiments of the Greeks; and in histories that documented the lives of his own tribal ancestors in England and Wales.

A Basic Right

Once the Revolutionary War was over, and the Constitution had been worked out and presented to the states for ratification, Jefferson turned his attention to what he and Madison felt was a terrible inadequacy in the new Constitution: It didn't explicitly stipulate the natural rights of the new nation's citizens, and didn't protect against the rise of new commercial monopolies like the East India Company.

On December 20, 1787, Jefferson wrote to James Madison about his concerns regarding the Constitution. He said bluntly that it was deficient in several areas. "I will now tell you what I do not like," he wrote. "First, the omission of a bill of rights, providing clearly, and without the aid of sophism, for freedom of religion, freedom of the press, protection against standing armies, restriction of monopolies, the eternal and unremitting force of the habeas corpus laws, and trials by jury in all matters of fact triable by the laws of the land, and not by the laws of nations."

Such a bill protecting natural persons from out-of-control governments or commercial monopolies shouldn't just be limited to America, Jefferson believed. "Let me add," he summarized, "that a bill of rights is what the people are entitled to against every government on earth, general or particular; and what no just government should reuse, or rest on inference."

In 1788, Jefferson wrote about his concerns to several people. In a letter to Mr. A. Donald, on February 7, he defined

Legacy of the Founding Fathers

The people who founded this nation didn't fight a war so that they could have a couple of "citizen representatives" sitting in on meetings of the British East India Company. They carried out a revolution in order to be free of oppression: corporate, governmental, or otherwise; and to replace it with democratic self-government.

It seems that things have slipped a little. Today, as soon as any group or movement puts together a coherent critique of the role of corporations, tongues start clucking. Politicians, mainstream reformers, degreed experts, and media commentators fall all over each other in an effort to dismiss such clear, practical, focused thinking as mere "conspiracy theories" cooked up by unbalanced "crackpots."

They forget that 17th century political philosopher Thomas Hobbes called corporations "worms in the body politic." Adam Smith condemned them for their effect in curtailing "natural liberty." And most of the so-called "founding fathers" of this nation shared an opinion of corporations that today would earn them the label "lunatic fringe" from the same mainstream tongue-cluckers.

Jane Anne Morris,
Rachel's Environment & Health Weekly,
April 4, 1996.

the items that should be in a bill of rights. "By a declaration of rights, I mean one which shall stipulate freedom of religion, freedom of the press, freedom of commerce against monopolies, trial by juries in all cases, no suspensions of the habeas corpus, no standing armies. These are fetters against doing evil, which no honest government should decline."

Jefferson kept pushing for a law, written into the Constitution as an amendment, which would prevent companies from growing so large that they could dominate entire industries or have the power to influence the people's government.

On February 12, 1788, he wrote to Mr. Dumas about his pleasure that the U.S. Constitution was about to be ratified, but also expressed his concerns about what was missing from the Constitution. He was pushing hard for his own state to reject the Constitution if it didn't protect people from the dangers he foresaw. "With respect to the new Government," he wrote, "nine or ten States will probably have accepted by the end of this month. The others may oppose it. Virginia, I think, will be of this number. Besides other objections of less moment, she [Virginia] will insist on annexing a bill of rights to the new Constitution, i.e. a bill wherein the Government shall declare that, 1. Religion shall be free; 2. Printing presses free; 3. Trials by jury preserved in all cases; 4. No monopolies in commerce; 5. No standing army. Upon receiving this bill of rights, she will probably depart from her other objections; and this bill is so much to the interest of all the States, that I presume they will offer it, and thus our Constitution be amended, and our Union closed by the end of the present year."

By midsummer of 1788, things were moving along and Jefferson was helping his close friend James Madison write the Bill of Rights. On the last day of July, he wrote to Madison, "I sincerely rejoice at the acceptance of our new constitution by nine States. It is a good canvass, on which some strokes only want retouching. What these are, I think are sufficiently manifested by the general voice from north to south, which calls for a bill of rights. It seems pretty generally understood, that this should go to juries, habeas corpus, standing armies, printing, religion, and monopolies."

The following year, on March 13, he wrote to Francis Hopkinson about continuing objection to monopolies, "You say that I have been dished up to you as an anti-federalist, and ask me if it be just. My opinion was never worthy enough of notice to merit citing; but since you ask it, I will tell it to you. I am not a federalist.... What I disapproved from the first moment also, was the want of a bill of rights, to guard liberty against the legislative as well as the executive branches of the government; that is to say, to secure freedom in religion, freedom of the press, freedom from monopolies, freedom from unlawful imprisonment, freedom from a permanent military, and a trial by jury, in all cases determinable by the laws of the land."

All of Jefferson's wishes, except two, would soon come true. But not all of his views were shared universally.

Rise of a Corporate Aristocracy

Years later, on October 28, 1813, Jefferson would write to John Adams about their earlier disagreements over whether a government should be run by the wealthy and powerful few (the pseudo-aristoi), or a group of the most wise and capable people (the "natural aristocracy"), elected from the larger class of all Americans, including working people.

"The artificial aristocracy is a mischievous ingredient in government," Jefferson wrote to Adams, "and provision should be made to prevent its ascendancy. On the question, what is the best provision, you and I differ; but we differ as rational friends, using the free exercise of our own reason, and mutually indulging its errors. You think it best to put the pseudo-aristoi into a separate chamber of legislation [the Senate], where they may be hindered from doing mischief by their coordinate branches, and where, also, they may be a protection to wealth against the agrarian and plundering enterprises of the majority of the people. I think that to give them power in order to prevent them from doing mischief, is arming them for it, and increasing instead of remedying the evil."

Adams and the Federalists were wary of the common person (who Adams referred to as "the rabble"), and many subscribed to the Calvinist notion that wealth was a sign of certification or blessing from above and a certain minimum level of morality. Since the Senate of the United States was elected by the state legislatures (not by the voters themselves, until 1913) and entirely made up of wealthy men, it was mostly on the Federalist side. Jefferson and the Democratic Republicans disagreed strongly with the notion of a Senate made up of the wealthy and powerful.

"Mischief may be done negatively as well as positively," Jefferson wrote to Adams in the next paragraph of that 1813 letter, still arguing for a directly elected Senate. "Of this, a cabal in the Senate of the United States has furnished many proofs. Nor do I believe them necessary to protect the wealthy; because enough of these will find their way into every branch of the legislation, to protect themselves. . . . I think the best remedy is exactly that provided by all our constitutions, to leave to the citizens the free election and separation of the aristoi from the pseudo-aristoi, of the wheat from the chaff. In general they will elect the really good and wise. In some instances, wealth may corrupt, and birth blind them; but not in sufficient degree to endanger the society."

Jefferson's vision of a more egalitarian Senate—directly elected by the people instead of by state legislators—finally became law in 1913 with the passage of the Seventeenth Amendment, promoted by the Populist Movement and passed on a wave of public disgust with the corruption of the political process by giant corporations.

Almost all of his visions for a Bill of Rights—all except "freedom from monopolies in commerce" and his concern about a permanent army—were incorporated into the actual

Bill of Rights, which James Madison shepherded through Congress and was ratified December 15, 1791.

But the Federalists fought hard to keep "freedom from monopolies" out of the Constitution. And they won. The result was a boom for very large businesses in America in the 19th and 20th centuries, which arguably brought our nation and much of the world many blessings.

But . . . some of those same principles have also given unexpected influence to the very monopolies Jefferson had argued must be constrained from the beginning. The result has sometimes been the same kind of problem the Tea Party rebels had risked their lives to fight: a situation in which the government protects one competitor against all others, and against the will of the people whose money is at stake—along with their freedom of choice.

| "The more educated you are the more indoctrinated you are. And you believe you are being free and objective, whereas in fact you're just repeating state propaganda." |

A Criminal Corporate Elite Runs the Government and the Media

Noam Chomsky, Interviewed by Irene McGee

White-collar crimes can be committed only in societies that permit them, asserts Noam Chomsky, the interview subject in the following viewpoint. Chomsky argues that the government perpetrates white-collar crimes all the time, and the media's function is either to make these crimes palatable to the American public through salesmanship or omit mention of the illegal activities altogether. Chomsky notes that the point of most entertainment is designed to sell products to people from their childhoods onward, whether it is a presidential candidate, a Wall Street bailout, or toothpaste.

Noam Chomsky is a scientist, author, and lecturer, as well as professor emeritus of linguistics at the Massachusetts Institute of

Noam Chomsky, Interviewed by Irene McGee, "On Fake News and Other Societal Woes; Interview with Noam Chomsky," No One's Listening, KSFS Radio, December 7, 2005. Reproduced by permission.

Technology. Irene McGee is the radio host of No One's Listening, *a regular podcast series covering the mass media.*

As you read, consider the following questions:

1. According to Chomsky, what in the television industry is the conceptual difference between "content" and "fill"?

2. What are the distinctions Chomsky draws between U.S. presidential elections and those in Brazil?

3. What reasons does Chomsky suggest motivated England and the United States to excise George Orwell's original introduction to the novel *Animal Farm?*

*I*nterviewer: *So our show today is about video news releases.*

Chomsky: Video news releases?

Video news releases and fake news. I imagine you don't have time to watch much tv, since you've written 90 books but I think the reason you'd be so good for this show is because you could give a historical analysis of the print media.

Well there was a period, in the mid-19th century, that's the period of the freest press, both in England and in the US. And it's quite interesting to look back at it. Over the years, that's declined. It declined for two basic reasons. One reason is the increased capital that was required to run a competitive press. And as capital requirements increased, that of course led to a more corporatized media. The other effect is advertisement. In the 19th century, the United States had something kind of approximating a market system. Now we have nothing like a market—they may teach you [that] in economics courses, but that's not the way it works. And one of the signs of the decline of the market is advertisement. So if you have a real market you don't advertise: you just give information. For example, there are corners of the economy that do run like markets—for example, stock markets. If you have ten shares of General Motors [GM] that you want to sell, you don't put up an ad on television with a sexy model holding up the ten shares saying "ask your broker if this is good for you; it's good for me," or something like that. What you do is you sell it at the market price. If you had a market for cars, toothpaste, or whatever, lifestyle drugs, you would do the same thing. GM would put up a brief notice saying here's the information about our models. Well, you've seen television ads, so I don't have to tell you how it works. The idea is to delude and deceive people with imagery. And the same has happened to the print media. Take the *New York Times* for example. They have something called the news hole. When the editors lay out tomorrow's newspapers, the first thing they do is the important things—they put the ads around. Then they have a little bit left that's called the news hole, and they stick little things there. Quite apart from that, the media are just big corporations and of course represent the interests of their owners, their markets, which are advertisers, and for the elite newspapers, more or less the managerial class, the educated population they deal with. The end result is that you get a very narrow perspective of what the world is like.

Well then, what would be the alternative? That's where I'm searching.

The alternative would be a free press. It's not hard to imagine, there actually was one in the mid-nineteenth century. So that would mean a press that isn't reliant on massive capital concentration, corporate ownership, that is not reliant on advertising for its revenue, and would involve engaged people who are interested in understanding the world and participating in a reasoned discussion about what it should be like. I mean, that's not inconceivable.

Right. I don't know if you know how these video news releases work. There are actually PR [public relations] agencies that don't try to be covert about it. They'll be called VNR PR agency.

It's very open. Take, say, television. In the industry they have an hour of program, whatever it is, a comedy, a cop show, or whatever. In the industry there's what's called content and fill. The content is the advertising. The fill is the car chase or the sex scene or something that's supposed to keep you going between ads. And if you look at a television program, actually I do it some times because I'm intrigued, the creativity and the imagination and the expenses and so on are for the ads; the car chase you can pull off the shelf. And in fact this has led to a serious deterioration of the political system. I mean we don't have anything resembling a democracy anymore. Take a look at the last campaign. The campaign is run by the same people who sell toothpaste, exactly the same PR agencies. And when they sell a candidate, they do it the exact same way they sell a lifestyle drug. You don't put up information about the candidate, what you do is create delusional images that delude and deceive. The population knows it. A very small number of the population, about 10% of the voters, literally, knew the stands of the candidates on the issues. And it's not because they are stupid or uninterested. It's just like you don't know the characteristics of toothpaste.

Hopefully we can change that and people can start questioning.

There's really two separate questions about the media, which are usually muddled. One is what they're trying to do and the second one is what's the effect on the public. The effect on the public isn't very much studied but to the extent that it has been, it seems as though among the more educated sectors the indoctrination works more effectively. Among the less educated sectors people are just more skeptical and cynical.

So what can we do now because I'm depressed.

Well, look, I think it's a very optimistic future, frankly.

Really?

Yes, very much so. There's something we know about the country, this country, more than any other. We know a lot about public opinion, it's studied very intensively. The results are very rarely reported but you can find them. It's an open society and you can find them. What they show is remarkable. What they show first of all is that both political parties and the media are far to the right of the general population on a whole host of issues and the population is just disorganized, atomized and so on. This country ought be an organizers' paradise. And that's why the media and the campaigns keep away from issues. They know that on issues they're going to lose people. So therefore you have to portray George Bush as a—look he's a pampered kid from a rich family who went to prep school and elite university, and you have to present him as an ordinary guy, who makes grammatical errors—which I'm sure he's trained to make, he didn't talk that way at Yale— fake Texas twang, and he's off to his ranch to, you know, cut brush or something.

Right, to go fishing.

That's like a toothpaste ad and I think a lot of people know it. Given the facts about public opinion, it means what's needed is something not very radical. Let's become as democratic as say the second largest country in the hemisphere, Brazil. I mean their last election was not between two rich kids who went to the same elite university and joined the same secret society where they're trained to be members of the upper class and they can get into politics because they have rich families with a lot of connections. I mean people were actually able to elect a president from their own ranks. A man who was a peasant union leader, never had a higher education, and comes from the population. They could do it because it's a functioning democratic society. I mean there were tremendous obstacles, repressive state, huge concentration of wealth, much worse obstacles than we have. But they have mass popular movements. They have actual political parties,

The Media's Selective Truth

The press functions as an important site for the production and dissemination of "truth." Mediated knowledge, whereby lived experience is transmitted to news narrative, is usually accomplished via routine electronic or print-based media systems and depends on a number of distinct but interrelated factors that are extrinsic to an event's seriousness: geopolitical interests, market needs, advertising policies, organizational budgets, access to and control of information sources, cultural priorities and newsworthiness, and dominant discourses that enable, guide, and sustain news coverage. On the one side are investments, markets, conglomerates, and monopolies; on the other side are lobby groups, political agendas, and the power to censure. Moreover, news making is also guided by intrinsic factors: editorial politics, story screening, the rhythms of the newsroom, the subculture of journalism, and cognitive conceptions of "audience interest" are all designed to shape the discursive content of the sayable. Reporters typically over-represent the harm and criminality of those most vulnerable to authoritative labelling and under-represent the harms caused by the powerful. As [journalists] Sandra Evans and Richard Lundman observed two decades ago, "newspapers protect corporate reputations by failing to provide frequent, prominent and criminally oriented coverage of common corporate crimes". When business crime is reported, it tends to be concentrated in up-market newspapers or on specialist pages and to be framed in ways that demarcate it from "real" crime.

John McMullen,
Canadian Journal of Criminology and Criminal Justice,
October 2006.

which we don't have. There's nothing to stop us from doing that. I mean we have a legacy of freedom which is unparalleled. It's been won by struggle over centuries, it was never given, and you can use it, or you can abandon it. It's a choice.

But don't you think to some extent maybe people don't even realize their own discontent because of the media?

No, I think people are very discontented and their attitudes towards the media are very cynical and skeptical.

The attitudes towards the media [are skeptical] but because we're not banding together they almost feel that sort of detachment. They don't know where to get angry or who to band with.

That's true. But that's again the lack of democratic structures. I mean if you have popular movements . . . Well, why are unions so detested by elites? Because unions are one of the few ways in which people without great privilege, working people, can actually get together—for workers' education, for interaction, for participation in the political arena and so on. So therefore they have to be destroyed. It's true that it's a very atomized society, and there are a lot of reasons for that. The last 25 years things have gotten much worse. The U.S. has gone through a unique period of economic history. Real wages for the majority of the population have stagnated or declined. Working hours have gone way up—they're now the highest in the industrial world, wages are the lowest. And people are deluged from infancy. You know, I watch children's television with my grandchildren sometimes. From practically infancy you are deluged with propaganda that says your life depends, your value as a human being depends, on how many useless commodities you consume. So you have a working family, you know, husband and wife, working to keep food on the table, their kids want to buy everything there is even though they don't need it or want it. Then you go deeply in debt and then you're trapped. You don't have time to talk to people—you don't know what your neighbors think. Popular attitudes are just not reported. Sometimes it's fantastic. So after the federal

235

budget came out last February [2005], the major public opinion institute in the country did a careful poll of people's attitudes toward the budget. It was just like a mirror image of what the budget was. Where federal spending is going up— military, Iraq, Afghanistan—people wanted it to go down, large majorities; where it was going down, same large majorities, people wanted it to go up: social spending, education, renewable energy, support for the United Nations, [and] so on. A huge majority wants Bush to rescind tax cuts for the rich, people with over $200,000 income and so on. Well how was that reported? Well a friend of mine did a database search and nothing. Zero. Only one newspaper in the country—some small town newspaper in Iowa.

So what's going on? Are they scared? I mean I've interviewed some journalists on this show and . . .

Look, they've just internalized the values. They'll tell you, and they're correct, that nobody is ordering them to do anything. That's right. Nobody is ordering them to do anything. The indoctrination is so deep that educated people think they're being objective. Actually this is a point that Orwell made. You and everybody else has read *Animal Farm*, I'm sure, but you and everybody else hasn't read the introduction to Animal Farm. There's a good reason for that: because it was suppressed. The introduction was found 30 years later in Orwell's own published papers. The introduction to *Animal Farm* says, look, this book is a satire on a totalitarian state but I'm going to talk about England, Free England. In Free England it's not that different. Without state coercion unpopular ideas can be suppressed and are. And then he described how. He didn't go in much details [sic] but he said partly it's because the press is owned by wealthy men who have every reason not to want certain ideas to be expressed. But the more important reason, he said, was because of a good education. By the time you've gone through, you know, Oxford and Cambridge and here you could say Harvard and Princeton and so on, and even less fancy places, you have instilled into you the understanding that there are certain things that [it] just wouldn't do to say, and that's what a good deal of education is. So the people who come out of it—and there are many filters—if people go off and try to be too critical there are many ways of discouraging them or eliminating them one way or the other. Some get through, it's not a uniform story. There are plenty of journalists with integrity and honesty. And many of them, some personal friends, will give a much harsher picture of the media than I do, because they have to live with it. But the basic points that Orwell made are fundamentally correct. The more educated you are the more indoctrinated you are. And you believe you are being free and objective, whereas in fact you're just repeating state propaganda.

I feel like one of the things with academic readings is that you can trace the source.

Well, for example, you could trace what I just told you about popular attitudes about the budget. But the point is that you have to do an individual research project, and who's going to do that? So some guy comes home from his 50 hour [work] week, his wife is working 50 hours, the kids are demanding this and that, does he have time to do an individual research project? That's what popular associations are for. When you have unions, political parties, women's groups, whatever it may be, people can get together and do those sorts of things. Individuals can't do them.

Well, that's what we're trying to do over here. I think that's one of the problems with the media . . .

The truth of the matter is NPR [National Public Radio] is not that different. So I listen to NPR when I'm driving for as long as I can stand it, that's supposed to be the liberal media, just take a look at their reporting. So last night I was listening to the reporting on Bush's speech about how to get victory in Iraq. Just imagine—just do a thought experiment. Suppose you were in Russia under [Leonid] Brezhnev or let's say in the early 80s and you heard reports about the war in Afghanistan. Well, I'm sure it would have been the same thing. They would have discussed how can we get victory, how can we destroy the terrorists, will this tactic work, will that tactic work, we're losing too many soldiers and so on. Well, just like the most liberal journal in the U.S. Did anybody ask the question in Russia: do we have a right to invade another country? Can you imagine anyone asking that question here? But in Russia there's a difference. That was totalitarian control, if you said the wrong thing you'd go off to the gulag. Here it's just willing subordination to power.

I think it's because what makes it through the filter is the only thing people see, so they latch onto that and don't even know to question other things . . .

It's indoctrination so profound that educated people can't even understand the question that I just raised. Try it with journalists. Ask them: can there be journalism on the Iraq war that can be something different from the college newspaper cheering for the home team?

Right. Yeah, I don't know.

Ask. There can't be because they can't think of it. It's like Orwell said: it's just inculcated into you that there are certain things that it wouldn't do to think.

But there are ways, that's what's so exciting about the Internet.

And there are plenty of opportunities.

> *"There are several problems with a conspiratorial view that don't fit with what we know about power structures."*

A Corporate Conspiracy Is a Myth

G. William Domhoff

While many believe that the media and the government are simply two branches of a single entity that controls the populace, G. William Domhoff argues in the following viewpoint that in reality such a system would be hard to maintain for long without being discovered.

Domhoff notes that such organization is beyond the means or motives of any bureaucracy, and that although the number of power brokers is far too large to support such a system, even historic incidents associated with conspiracies, from the Kennedy assassination to 9/11, were conducted by individuals with no linkage to corporate power networks.

G. William Domhoff is a research professor at the University of California, Santa Cruz. He is the author of The Power Elite and the State: How Policy Is Made in America *and* Who Rules America: Power, Politics, and Social Change.

G. William Domhoff, "Theories of Power: There Are No Conspiracies," *Who Rules America*, March 2005. Reproduced by permission.

As you read, consider the following questions:

1. What does the author consider a basic flaw of the conspiratorial view when it comes to gauging the psychology and education of presumed "behind-the-scenes leaders"?

2. In Domhoff's opinion what is flawed about the notion of power residing in the hands of only a few dozen people?

3. What are two examples the author gives of illegal actions on the part of the U.S. government that do not qualify as conspiracies?

Many people seem to believe that America is ruled from behind the scenes by a conspiratorial elite with secret desires, i.e., by a small secretive group that wants to change the government system or put the country under the control of a world government. In the past, the conspirators were usually said to be secret Communist sympathizers who were intent upon bringing the United States under a common world government with the Soviet Union, but the collapse of the Soviet Union in 1991 undercut that theory. So most conspiratorial theorists changed their focus to the United Nations as the likely controlling force in a "new world order," an idea which is undermined by the powerlessness of the United Nations and the unwillingness of even moderates within the American power structure to give it anything but a limited role.

For a smaller group of conspiratorial thinkers, a secret group of operatives located within the CIA was responsible for many terrible tragedies and assassinations since the 1960s, including the assassination of President John F. Kennedy.

Problems with a Conspiratorial View

There are several problems with a conspiratorial view that don't fit with what we know about power structures. First, it assumes that a small handful of wealthy and highly educated people somehow develop an extreme psychological desire for power that leads them to do things that don't fit with the roles they seem to have. For example, that rich capitalists are no longer out to make a profit, but to create a one-world government. Or that elected officials are trying to get the constitution suspended so they can assume dictatorial powers. These kinds of claims go back many decades now, and it is always said that it is really going to happen this time, but it never does. Since these claims have proved wrong dozens of times by now, it makes more sense to assume that leaders act for their usual reasons, such as profit-seeking motives and institutionalized roles as elected officials. Of course they want to make as much money as they can, and be elected by huge margins every time, and that can lead them to do many unsavory things, but nothing in the ballpark of creating a one-world government or suspending the constitution.

Second, the conspiratorial view assumes that the behind-the-scenes leaders are extremely clever and knowledgeable, whereas social science and historical research shows that leaders often make shortsighted or mistaken decisions due to the limits placed on their thinking by their social backgrounds and institutional roles. When these limits are exposed through stupid mistakes, such as the failure of the CIA at the Bay of Pigs during the Kennedy Administration, then conspiratorial theorists assert that the leaders failed on purpose to fool ordinary people.

Third, the conspiratorial view places power in the hands of only a few dozen or so people, often guided by one strong leader, whereas sociologists who study power say that there is a leadership group of many thousands for a set of wealth-owning families that numbers several million. Furthermore, the sociological view shows that the groups or classes below the highest levels buy into the system in various ways and support it. For example, highly trained professionals in medicine, law, and academia have considerable control over their own lives, make a good living, and usually enjoy their work, so they go along with the system even though they do not have much political power.

Fourth, the conspiratorial view often assumes that clever experts ("pointy-headed intellectuals") with bizarre and grandiose ideas have manipulated the thinking of their hapless bosses. But studies of policy-making suggest that experts work within the context of the values and goals set out by the leaders, and that they are ignored or replaced if they step outside the consensus (which is signaled by saying they have become overly abstract, idealistic, or even, frankly, "pinko" [a slang term for showing Communist leanings]).

Finally, the conspiratorial view assumes that illegal plans to change the government or assassinate people can be kept secret for long periods of time, but all evidence shows that secret groups or plans in the United States are uncovered by civil liberties groups, infiltrated by reporters or government officials, and written about in the press. Even secrets about wars and CIA operations—Vietnam, the Contras, the rationales for [George W.] Bush's invasion of Iraq in 2003—are soon exposed for everyone to see. As for assassinations and assassination attempts in the United States, from [Presidents] McKinley to Franklin D. Roosevelt to John F. Kennedy to Martin Luther King, Jr., to Robert F. Kennedy to [Ronald] Reagan, they have been the acts of individuals with no connections to any power groups.

Because all their underlying assumptions are discredited by historical events and media exposures, no conspiracy theory is credible on any issue. If there is corporate domination, it is through leaders in visible positions within the corporate community, the policy planning network, and the government. If there is class domination, it is through the same mundane processes that social scientists have shown to be operating for other levels of the socioeconomic system.

Traits of Populist Conspiracies

[Author] Margaret Canovan argues: All forms of populism "involve some kind of exaltation of and appeal to 'the people,' and all are in one sense or another antielitist." We take these two elements—celebration of "the people" plus some form of antielitism—as a working definition of populism. A populist movement—as opposed, for example, to one-shot populist appeals in an election campaign—uses populist themes to mobilize a mass constituency as a sustained political or social force. . . .

Michael Kazin calls populism a style of organizing. Populist movements can be on the right, the left, or in the center. They can be egalitarian or authoritarian, and can rely on decentralized networks or a charismatic leader. They can advocate new social and political relations or romanticize the past. Especially important for our purposes, populist movements can promote forms of antielitism that target either genuine structures of oppression or scapegoats alleged to be part of a secret conspiracy. And they can define "the people" in ways that are inclusive and challenge traditional hierarchies, or in ways that silence or demonize oppressed groups.

Chip Berlet,
Right-Wing Populism in America, *2000.*

Attempts to Deceive the Public

Even though there are no conspiracies, it is also true that government officials sometimes take illegal actions or try to deceive the public. During the 1960s, for example, government leaders claimed that the Vietnam War was easily winnable, even though they knew otherwise. In the 1980s the Reagan

Administration defied a Congressional ban on support for anti-government rebels in Nicaragua (the "Contras") through a complicated scheme that raised money for the rebels from foreign countries. The plan included an illegal delivery of armaments to Iran in exchange for money and hostages. But deceptions and illegal actions are usually uncovered, if not immediately, then in historical records.

In the case of the Vietnam War deception, the unauthorized release in 1971 of government documents called The Pentagon Papers (which revealed the true state of affairs) caused the government great embarrassment and turned more people against the war. It also triggered the creation of a secret White House operation to plug leaks (the "Plumbers"), which led in turn to an illegal entry into Democratic Party headquarters [Watergate] during the 1972 elections, an attempted cover-up of high-level approval of the operation, and the resignation of President Richard M. Nixon in the face of impeachment charges. As for the Reagan Administration's illegal activities, they were unraveled in widely viewed Congressional hearings that led to a six-month imprisonment for the president's National Security Adviser for his part in an unsuccessful cover-up, along with convictions or guilty pleas for several others for obstruction of justice or lying to Congress. The Secretary of Defense was indicted for his part in the cover-up, but spared a trial when he was pardoned by President George H.W. Bush on Christmas Eve, 1992.

It is also true that the CIA has been involved in espionage, sabotage, and the illegal overthrow of foreign governments, and that the FBI spied on and attempted to disrupt Marxist third parties, the Civil Rights Movement, and the Ku Klux Klan. But careful studies show that all these actions were authorized by top government officials, which is the critical point here. There was no "secret team" or "shadow government" committing illegal acts or ordering government officials to deceive the public and disrupt social movements. Such a distinction is crucial in differentiating all sociological theories of power from a conspiratorial one.

The group said by many conspiratorial thinkers to be at the center of the alleged conspiracy in the United States, the Council on Foreign Relations [CFR], is in fact a mere policy discussion forum. It has nearly 3,000 members, far too many for secret plans to be kept within the group. All the CFR does is sponsor discussion groups, debates and speakers. As far as being secretive, it issues annual reports and allows access to its historical archives. Historical studies of the CFR show that it has a very different role in the overall power structure than what is claimed by conspiratorial theorists.

"*Most business sections of daily papers seldom apply to corporations the same criteria of validation and critical judgment applied to other subjects.*"

As Large Corporations Themselves the Media Underreport White-Collar Crime

Ben H. Bagdikian

Although the First Amendment of the Constitution guarantees freedom of the press to investigate corporate wrongdoings, many newspapers are now owned by conglomerates as large as the companies on whose actions they are reporting, and in some cases by the same corporations themselves. Ben H. Bagdikian, the author of the following viewpoint, argues that such synergy has a direct, corrupting effect on how corporations, and corporate crimes, are portrayed in the popular media. Bagdikian asserts that in the modern power structure, investigative reporters who attempt to run stories critical of big corporations tend to be punished rather than rewarded for their tenacity.

Ben H. Bagdikian is a former journalism professor at the Univesity of California, Berkeley and a Pulitzer Prize–winning journalist. His books include In The Midst of Plenty: The Poor in America *and* The Effete Conspiracy, and Other Crimes by the Press.

As you read, consider the following questions:

1. According to the author, what are two examples of public anger at corporate behavior expressed since 1970?
2. In Bagdikian's view, what special advantages do corporations enjoy over the media?
3. What does the author claim is the real aim of corporate advertising?

Almost all news media have friends who are given preferential treatment in the news, who are immune to criticism, who can keep out embarrassing information, or who are guaranteed a positive image. In the newsrooms of America, these friends are called "sacred cows." They frequently include the owner, the owner's family and friends, major advertisers, and the owner's political causes. Sacred cows in the news run the gamut from petunias to presidents. In one northeastern city the sacred cow is civic flowerbeds donated by the publisher's spouse; in another city it is an order that any picture of Richard Nixon must show him smiling.

The sacred cows in American newsrooms leave residues common to all cows. But no sacred cow has been so protected and has left more generous residues in the news than the American corporation. So it is ironic that in the last decade the most bitter attacks on the news media have come from the American corporate system. The irony becomes exquisite when, in the 1980s, the segment of American life that most hates the news increasingly comes to own it.

Large classes of people are ignored in the news, are reported as exotic fads, or appear only at their worst—minorities, blue-collar workers, the lower middle class, the poor. They become publicized mainly when they are in spectacular accidents, go on strike, or are arrested. Other groups and in-stitutions—government, schools, universities, and non-established political movements—are subjected to periodic criticism. Minor tribes like athletes, fashion designers, and ac-tors receive routine praise. But since World War I hardly a mainstream American news medium has failed to grant its most favored treatment to corporate life.

There has been much to celebrate in the history of corpo-rate industry and technology. Great cities rose and flourished, material goods flowed to the populace, cash spread to new classes of people, standards of living rose, and life was pro-longed in developed countries.

There have also been ugliness and injustice in corporate wielding of power—bloody repressions of workers who tried to organize unions, corruption of government, theft of public franchises. But through it all, most of the mass media de-picted corporate life as benevolent and patriotic. . . .

Promoters of the Corporate Ethic

In most walks of public life, corporations are accustomed to a smooth path edged with indulgence. Criticism in the United States had tended to be short-lived if it came from govern-ment or established sources. Longer-lasting criticism came from public health authorities, social scientists, union, liberal and left activists, and other specialized voices. In both cases, either criticism failed to be reported in the mass media or the reports were brief or even neutralized by the media's criticism of the critics.

The standard media—mainstream newspapers, magazines, and broadcasters—had always been reliable promoters of the corporate ethic. Whole sections of newspapers were always de-voted to unrelieved glorification of business people, not just in advertisements where corporations pay for self-praise but in "news" that is assumed to be dispassionate. Most business sections of daily papers seldom apply to corporations the same criteria of validation and critical judgment applied to other subjects. Most business pages consist of corporate propaganda in the form of press releases run without significant changes or printed verbatim. Each day millions of expensive pages of stock market quotations are printed, even though only a small minority of American households actively trade in the stock market. Editorially, corporate causes almost invariably become news media causes. Among the most commonly suppressed news items each year are stories involving corporations that are reported in the major media. The integration of corporate values into the national pieties could not have been established without prolonged indoctrination by the main body of American news organizations.

In the years after 1970, mounting public anger at some corporate behavior does occasionally find expression in print and on the air, as when the public was asked to sacrifice warm homes and car travel during a gas shortage while the major oil companies reported their highest profits in history. Or local demonstrations against polluting industries became melodrama that met the criteria for conflict news. Or a spectacular trial, like the Ford Motor Company defense against criminal charges of neglect for its defective Pinto gas tanks, caught the media's attention. The barriers against damaging news about corporations were high but not impassable. Journalism had slowly changed so that in a few standard media, including, ironically, the daily bible of business, the *Wall Street Journal,* there were more than brief flurries of items about bad public performances of big business. There was still no significant criticism of the corporate system, simply reporting of isolated cases, but for the first time there was a breach in the almost uniform litany of unremitting praise and promotion of corporate behavior.

Corporate leaders were outraged. They criticized government agencies that reported corporate culpability. In their political action committees they raised the largest campaign war chests in electoral history to defeat candidates they considered hostile to business, and in 1980 they elected a national administration dedicated to wiping out half a century of social legislation and regulation of business. They created intellectual think tanks to counter academic studies damaging to corporations. But the corporations reserved their greatest wrath for the news media. Hell hath no fury like the sacred cow desanctified.

Business vs. the Media

Business had special advantages in its attack on the media. It had privileged access to media executives through common corporate associations and lobbies, and it could produce large-scale advertisements to counter antibusiness news and, increasingly, to use as threats of withdrawal against hostile media. And corporate leaders could invoke against the media that peculiar American belief (ironically created more by the media than by any other source) that to criticize big business is to attack American democracy.

Criticizing the media is neither unnatural nor harmful. The difference in the corporate attack was that the campaign attempted to discredit the whole system of American news as subversive to American values and to characterize journalists as a class of careless "economic illiterates" biased against business.

Some specific corporate complaints were justified. Throughout journalism there is more carelessness and sloth than should be tolerated. Most reporters are "economic illiterates" in the sense that they lack skills to analyze business records and they seldom have the sophistication to comprehend world economic forces. But the accusation that standard American reporting was biased against business was absurd. . . .

No other news sources, including high government officials, have been as effective as corporate executives in causing reporters to be fired, demoted, or removed from their beats. If the routine reporting of negative news about business from official sources was enraging, the idea of journalists taking the initiative in their own investigation of business, as they do with government, welfare recipients, and organized crime, tended to produce hysteria.

Overzealous Reporters

Leonard Matthews, president of the American Association of Advertising Agencies, said that "business and the entire free enterprise system need to be supported by the media" but that this "mutually healthy relationship" had been "impaired in recent years by the overzealous actions of a small but very visible group of investigative reporters who have made a practice of slugging advertisers while their associates in the sales department were accepting an order from the same company."

In the 1980s there were more investigative reporters than ever before. They had their own organization, Investigative Reporters and Editors. And the stereotype of the journalist as radical and antibusiness does not match the facts. An authoritative study by Stephen Hess showed that 58 percent of Washington correspondents consider themselves "middle of the road" or "conservative" politically. "In the past," Hess wrote, "the Washington press corps was liberal . . . a stereotype of the news corps that is no longer accurate."

It does not excuse journalists, who should become competent in the subjects they cover, but genuine economic literacy throughout the American population is remarkably low for a society in which economics has become the center of national politics. It is even more remarkable that business people themselves are among the most economically illiterate. A survey of three thousand persons by the business-oriented Advertising Council showed that "only 8% of all U.S. businessmen can

Number of Corporations that Control a Majority of U.S. Media

(newspaper, magazines, TV and radio stations, books, music, movies, videos, wire services and photo agencies)

Statistics reveal that the number of corporations controlling U.S. media outlets over the past 25 years has dwindled dramatically into an extremely small and powerful handful.

TAKEN FROM: http://www.corporations.org/media/.

correctly define the functions of these five groups—business, labor, the consumer, the investor, and advertising." . . .

Corporations as Heroes

Perhaps nowhere is the cynicism more blatant than in the newly energized activity known as corporate advertising. This constitutes printed and broadcast ads designed not to sell goods and services but to promote the politics and benevolent image of the corporation—and to attack anything that spoils the image. Ideology-image ads as a category of all ads doubled in the 1970s and had become a half-billion dollar-a-year enterprise.

The head of a large advertising agency described the purpose:

> It presents the corporation as hero, a responsible citizen, a force for good, presenting information on the work the company is doing in community relations, assisting the less fortunate, minimizing pollution, controlling drugs, ameliorating poverty.

The publication *Media Decisions* estimated that as much as $3 billion in corporate money goes into all methods of promoting the corporation as hero and into "explanations of the capitalistic system," including massive use of corporate books and teaching materials in the schools, almost all tax deductible. . . .

Oil Versus a Journalist

The quiet power of a large corporation to suppress damaging information and to silence the journalist who brings it to light can be seen in the attack by Mobil and its oil industry allies on an economics reporter for United Press International (UPI), then a leading American news agency.

Major oil companies based in the United States pay an extremely low U.S. income tax. The meager percentages are obscured by oil industry finances that are so arcane that even the Securities and Exchange Commission has said that they cannot be dealt with by ordinary accounting methods. But when the complexities of industry finances were expressed in plain language, Mobil and its friends decided to discredit the correspondent who accomplished the task.

The reporter selected for treatment was a poor example of the corporate stereotype of a liberal-radical journalist hostile to business. Edward F. Roby of UPI is a graduate of West Point, was awarded a Silver Star for Vietnam combat, is a devotee of conservative economist Milton Friedman, and personally believes that corporations should pay no income taxes. But he also believes in reporting the news and making it clear.

On June 5, 1981, Roby received a routine government report in the Washington bureau of UPI. It was a study of oil company revenues and taxes prepared by the Financial Reporting System of the U.S. Department of Energy. He noticed that the effective tax rate for the twenty-six largest energy firms, including Mobil, Exxon, and Gulf, was surprisingly low for the adjusted gross income. The adjusted gross income for the oil companies was the income of the parent firm within the United States after the firm had been forgiven U.S. taxes for any taxes paid in other countries.

The nominal corporate income tax was 46 percent, but in fact the average tax paid by all U.S. corporations in 1979 was 23.7 percent. The twenty-six largest energy companies, according to the report, paid even less—12.4 percent—at a time of record-high oil industry profits. The 12.4 percent income tax rate for the biggest oil company was, Roby learned from the Internal Revenue Service, the same rate that would be paid by a private citizen who made less than twenty thousand dollars a year. He wrote that information in a story that appeared on UPI news wires in June 1981.

Shortly after Roby's story went out on the wires, a Mobil ad appeared in "the Mobil position" in eleven influential American newspapers under the headline: Won't They Ever Learn? "Once again," the ad began, "newspaper readers across the country were recently presented with a massive dose of misinformation on oil industry taxes."

After its usual denunciation of a news article about oil profits being "misleading" and "blatantly incorrect," the Mobil ad concluded, "This is not the first time the oil industry has been falsely accused of underpaying its taxes ... we hope that UPI will set the record straight so the American public can make judgments based on accurate and reliable data."

The ad told readers that oil company income is

taxed by the country in which it is earned according to the country's corporate tax rate. These foreign income taxes—

and only income taxes—are credited by U.S. law against taxes on that foreign income to avoid double taxation on the same income. . . . Despite the fact that we have pointed it out hundreds of times, reporters still can't seem to get it right.

But Roby and UPI were correct. . . .

Tony Dinigro, media manager for Mobil Oil, told a meeting sponsored by the right-wing group Accuracy in the Media that the "Won't They Ever Learn?" ad was designed to embarrass the wire services. Dinigro said, "We hope this ad will serve to put the reporter, the wire service and other reporters who are writing about this subject—about Mobil—on notice to make sure they take the time to . . . do an accurate piece."

The concerted attack on Roby worked. UPI told him to do no further stories about Mobil and no in-depth stories on oil and taxes, even though his specialty in the UPI Washington bureau was energy and environment and even though his superiors agreed that his stories about the oil companies had been accurate. Shortly afterward, Roby left UPI and became a European correspondent for another major American news organization.

Why did [Mobil] pick on Roby when the same passage was reported independently by papers like the *Wall Street Journal*, the *Washington Post*, and other news organizations? One possibility is that Roby's story about all oil company income taxes had made him a target.

An object lesson in the Corporate School of Journalism had been given. Corporations have multimillion-dollar budgets to dissect and attack news reports they dislike. But with each passing year they have yet another power: They are not only hostile to independent journalists. They are their employers.

On October 19, 1981, UPI dutifully reported another attack on American news media. A corporate executive said:

"What our country needs worse than anything is freedom from the press. . . . The press is absolutely intolerable today."

The speaker was Arthur Temple. Temple at the time was vice chairman of Temple-Eastex, which was the largest single stockholder in Time, Inc., the largest magazine publisher in the country and employer of hundreds of journalists whom Mr. Temple, then a director at Time, Inc., considered "absolutely intolerable." Among the publications over which Mr. Temple had responsibilities, as a director, was a major reporter on American business, *Fortune* magazine.

Periodical Bibliography

Miriam H. Baer — "Linkage and the Deterrence of Corporate Fraud," *Virginia Law Review*, October 2008.

Sara Sun Beale — "Is Corporate Criminal Liability Unique?" *American Criminal Law Review*, Fall 2007.

Darren Bush and Carrie Mayne — "In (Reluctant) Defense of Enron," *Oregon Law Review*, vol. 83, 2004.

Charlie Cray — "The Government's Business," *Multinational Monitor*, May-June 2004.

Malcolm Gladwell — "Open Secrets," *New Yorker*, January 8, 2007.

Michael Goldsmith — "Resurrecting RICO: Removing Immunity for White-Collar Crime," *Harvard Journal on Legislation*, Winter 2004.

Vikramaditya S. Khanna — "Politics and Corporate Crime Legislation: If Politically Powerful Corporations Feared Corporate Crime Laws, Then Why Are So Many Statutes on the Books?" *Regulation*, Spring 2004.

Daniel T. Ostas — "Cooperate, Comply, or Evade? A Corporate Executive's Social Responsibilities with Regard to the Law," *American Business Law Journal*, Summer 2004.

Christopher Palmeri — "For the Feds, White-Collar Crime Pays," *Business Week*, March 20, 2006.

Vincenzo Ruggiero — "Privatizing International Conflict: War as Corporate Crime," *Social Justice*, Fall-Winter 2007.

Jane Schneider and Peter Schneider — "Power Projects: Comparing Corporate Scandal and Organized Crime," *Social Analysis*, Fall 2003.

For Further Discussion

Chapter 1

1. Ted Nace charges that corporations by their nature are designed to sidestep the same financial laws imposed on them in a democratic society, while Edwin Meese asserts that the legality of corporate activities is only relevant in the event of a conviction. What are the differences and similarities between Nace's and Meese's arguments?

2. Stuart P. Green argues that what constitutes white-collar crime is open to debate as a result of changing laws and mores, while Harry Glasbeek argues that stealing money is objectively wrong regardless of the circumstances or income levels of the principals. How well does each author make his case?

Chapter 2

1. Linda Wasmer Andrews asserts that white-collar criminals do not need to be wealthy to be guilty of white-collar crimes, while Cynthia Crossen suggests that the majority of white-collar criminals are wealthy to begin with. In what ways do both authors differentiate between individuals who commit identity theft and corporations guilty of financial misconduct?

2. Kenneth R. Gray, Larry A. Frieder, and George W. Clark, Jr., claim that ethics should be the cornerstone of any reputable business school's curriculum, drawing from numerous historical sources to bolster their argument. How large a role do you think the authors would contend that poor ethics played in the U.S. banking crisis that began in 2008? Explain.

3. Tom O'Connor believes that while most white-collar criminals carefully orchestrate their crimes in advance, at heart they tend to be psychologically impaired individuals who believe that they are not accountable for their actions. Neal Shover and Andy Hochstetler, however, argue that, due to its complexity, white-collar crime is necessarily a rational choice made by its perpetrators, which suggests a high level of mental stability. Do you agree or disagree with these authors? Which viewpoint do you consider better supported? Why?

Chapter 3

1. Nicole Gelinas believes that due to most people's lack of understanding of the intricacies of the business world, people of wealth are the victims of reverse discrimination. How do you think that Gelinas feels about the media's treatment of high-profile white-collar defendants like Bernard Madoff?

2. Ross Todd believes that recovering even a portion of the money owed by convicted white-collar criminals is improbable, considering the vast sums involved and already spent. From the tone Todd adopts, is he opposed to stiffer financial penalties for white-collar criminals or more lenient ones, and what do you think that Todd believes the solution is?

3. Brian K. Payne writes that many white-collar offenders end up doing prison time as a result of judicial efforts to "balance the scales" between rich and poor inmates. David Feige, on the other hand, argues that most white-collar criminals either go free or serve minimal sentences. Which author do you agree with? Whose viewpoint do you consider better supported? Why?

4. Due to the high speed and technical complexities of globalized commerce, Richard Johnston suggests that updated identity theft statistics are difficult to calculate with preci-

sion, which hampers the government's efforts to crack down on such cases. What reasons does Johnston provide to explain the government's apparent inability to keep up with Internet criminals technologically?

Chapter 4

1. Thom Hartmann claims that the United States was originally founded by leaders of independent colonies who deemed the notion of a ruling corporate monopoly oppressive. What examples does the author draw from history to support his case that the relationship between government and corporate enterprise has become steadily more problematic? In what ways does Hartmann suggest that this relationship has remained the same since the Revolutionary War?

2. Noam Chomsky argues that the government and the media are both controlled by a powerful corporate elite of wealthy individuals who directly affect public policy, as well as how such policies are defined and debated by news pundits. G. William Domhoff retorts that it would be statistically impossible for a single group to maintain effective control over so many outlets for any length of time. Which author do you think makes a better argument for his position and why?

3. Ben H. Bagdikian suggests that the TV and print news media consciously avoid reporting on scandals that might incriminate or embarrass the five corporations that control most American newspapers, magazines, and radio and television stations. What do you believe the author thinks about the Fairness Doctrine, which requires stations to devote equal time for opposing views in discussions of public issues? What might Bagdikian suggest is the inherent flaw in the Fairness Doctrine?

Organizations to Contact

The editors have compiled the following list of organizations concerned with the issues debated in this book. The descriptions are derived from materials provided by the organizations. All have publications or information available for interested readers. The list was compiled on the date of publication of the present volume; the information provided here may change. Be aware that many organizations take several weeks or longer to respond to inquiries, so allow as much time as possible.

American Institute of Certified Public Accountants (AICPA)
1211 Avenue of the Americas, New York, NY   10036
(888) 777-7077 • fax: (800) 362-5066
Web site: www.aicpa.org/antifraud

The American Institute of Certified Public Accountants is the outgrowth of an organization founded in 1887 designed to help the public better understand the process of accounting. It also gives the accounting industry a venue to represent its interests before governments, regulatory bodies, and other agencies. In addition to promoting public awareness and confidence in the integrity, objectivity, and competence of professional accountants, the AICPA also establishes ethical standards, assists members in improving their conduct, performance, and expertise, and monitors the industry to enforce current standards and requirements. Online resources range from a media center and video library to magazines and newsletters, mentoring guidelines, an antifraud resource center, and a peer review public file.

Association of Certified Fraud Examiners (ACFE)
716 West Ave., Austin, TX   78701-2727
(800) 245-3321
e-mail: research@acfe.com
Web site: www.acfe.com

The ACFE is a charitable organization that attempts to provide antifraud education through online resources and by organizing community events. It also supports the works of future antifraud professionals across the world through the funding of scholarships, research, endowments, and other educational projects. In addition to publishing a bimonthly print magazine, *Fraud*, the association's online tools range from prominent case studies and video downloads to sample documents and insights from antifraud professionals. There is also an extensive article archive, contact information for certified fraud examiners for consultation, a fraud prevention check-up, and access to *EthicsLine*, a confidential, anonymous fraud reporting service.

Ethics Resource Center
2345 Crystal Drive, Suite 201, Arlington, VA   22202
(703) 647-2185 • fax: (703) 647-2180
e-mail: nick@ethics.org
Web site: www.ethics.org

Founded in 1922, the Ethics Resource Center claims to be the oldest nonprofit in the United States devoted to the advancement of organizational ethics. Members meet twice a year to discuss ethical issues and initiate research related to understudied topics. The company also provides advisory services to organizations to assess their ethical compliance programs. Its online resources include a listing of articles, books and other publications written by ERC staff members and leaders, a resource database on ethics and global integrity, and an Ethics Toolkit that features answers to frequently asked ethical questions, practical ethics guides, and a timeline of business ethics over the past five decades.

Federal Bureau of Investigation (FBI)
J. Edgar Hoover Building, Washington, DC   20535-0001
(202) 324-3000
Web site: www.fbi.gov

The Federal Bureau of Investigation is a national government agency with investigative jurisdiction over more than two hundred categories of federal crime. Title 28 of the United States Code establishes the FBI's mandate to "detect . . . crimes against the United States," including mail fraud; bank fraud; fraud by wire, radio, or television; and other instances of major white-collar crime. Online resources include an electronic reading room, an unabridged version of the Freedom of Information Act, forms to request financial records online, and detailed lists of annual crime statistics. The site also features information on how to be "crime smart" by avoiding identity theft and securities scams.

Financial Crimes Enforcement Network (FinCEN)
(703) 905-3591
Web site: www.fincen.gov

The U.S. Department of the Treasury founded the Financial Crimes Enforcement Network as a government-wide financial analysis organization in 1990. Responsible for establishing and administering the Bank Secrecy Act, FinCEN authorizes the treasury secretary to require financial institutions to submit record-keeping information on demand. Its Web site features a description of key federal regulations and statutes, a timeline of how the Bank Secrecy Act has been employed since its inception, and detailed accounts of crackdowns on historic financial and Internet-related crimes.

The Legal Information Institute (LII)
Cornell Law School, Ithaca, NY   14853
Web site: www4.law.cornell.edu

The LII is a research and electronic publishing arm of the Cornell Law School and a provider of public legal information and opinions. Its Web site compiles existing U.S. laws and regulations and contains numerous resources, journals, and articles pertaining to white-collar crime cases. Resources include topical libraries on American legal ethics and federal rules of bankruptcy and evidence, as well as the full text of the national banking bailout and stimulus bills.

National White Collar Crime Center
10900 Nuckols Road, Suite 325, Glen Allen, VA   23060
(804) 323-3563, ext. 31 • fax: (804) 323-3566
Web site: www.nw3c.org

This nonprofit organization collects articles and resources devoted to studying and investigating economic crimes, particularly those involving cyberspace. The group specializes in providing training and research to students and law enforcement agencies involved in the prevention and detection of white-collar crime and publishes twice a year a magazine called *The Informant* that focuses on news and highlights related to economic and cyber-crime. Online facilities include an archive of information dedicated to education, forensic laboratory services, and other aspects of cyber-crime investigation.

U.S. Securities and Exchange Commission (SEC)
100 F Street NE, Washington, DC   20549
(202) 942-8088
e-mail: help@sec.gov
Web site: www.sec.gov

The U.S. Securities and Exchange Commission was formed by the United States government as part of the Securities Act of 1933 to help restore investor and public confidence in the stock markets. The SEC oversees key participants and transactions in the securities industry and promotes the disclosure of important market-related information, as well as attempting to maintain fair dealing and protecting against fraud. The SEC requires public companies to disclose meaningful financial information to the public and works closely with other institutions, including Congress, to bring hundreds of civil enforcement actions against individuals and companies for violations of corporate law every year. Online resources include a database of disclosure documents that public companies are required to file with the commission, as well as descriptions of current laws and regulations, requests for public documents, webcasts, speeches and public statements, a news digest, and a daily summary of recent SEC actions, including enforcement proceedings, rule filings, and policy statements.

Bibliography

Tom D. Bazley   *Investigating White-Collar Crime.*
Upper Saddle River, NJ:
Prentice-Hall, 2007.

Michael L.
Benson   *White-Collar Crime: An Opportunity Perspective*, Springfield, IL: Charles C. Thomas, 2006.

David Callahan   *The Cheating Culture: Why More Americans Are Doing Wrong to Get Ahead.* New York: Routledge, 2009.

Tracy Coenen   *Essentials of Corporate Fraud.* Hoboken, NJ: John Wiley & Sons, 2008.

James William
Coleman   *The Criminal Elite: Understanding White-Collar Crime.* New York: Worth, 2005.

Denis Collins   *Behaving Badly: Ethical Lessons from Enron.* Indianapolis: Dog Ear, 2006.

Mary Dodge   *Women and White Collar Crime.* Upper Saddle River, NJ: Prentice-Hall, 2008.

Kurt Eichenwald   *Conspiracy of Fools: A True Story.* New York: Broadway Books, 2005.

Jurg Gerber and
Eric L. Jensen,
eds.   *Encyclopedia of White-Collar Crime.* Westport, CT: Greenwood, 2006.

Harry Glasbeek	*Wealth by Stealth: Corporate Law, Corporate Crime, and the Perversion of Democracy*. Toronto: Between the Lines, 2002.
Terry L. Leap	*Dishonest Dollars: The Dynamics of White-Collar Crime*. Ithaca, NY: Cornell University Press, 2007.
John P. Minkes and Leonard Minkes, eds.	*Corporate and White Collar Crime.* Thousand Oaks, CA: Sage, 2008.
Carolyn Nordstrom	*Global Outlaws: Crime, Money, and Power in the Contemporary World.* Berkeley and Los Angeles: University of California Press, 2007.
Ellen S. Podgor and Jerold H. Israel	*White Collar Crime in a Nutshell*. St. Paul, MN: West, 2004.
Jeffrey Reiman	*The Rich Get Richer and the Poor Get Prison: Ideology, Class, and Criminal Justice*. 8th Ed. Boston: Allyn & Bacon, 2006.
Paul H. Robinson and Michael T. Cahill	*Law Without Justice: Why Criminal Law Doesn't Give People What They Deserve*. New York: Oxford University Press, 2006.
Stephen M. Rosoff, Henry N. Pontell, and Robert Tillman	*Profit Without Honor: White Collar Crime and the Looting of America* Upper Saddle River, NJ: Prentice-Hall, 2006.

Danny Schechter   *Plunder: Investigating Our Economic Calamity and the Subprime Scandal.* New York: Cosimo Books, 2008.

Sally S. Simpson   *Corporate Crime, Law, and Social Control.* New York: Cambridge University Press, 2002.

J. Kelly Strader   *Understanding White Collar Crime.* Albany, NY: LexisNexis/Matthew Bender, 2006.

David Weisburd, Elin Waring, and Ellen F. Chayet   *White-Collar Crime and Criminal Careers.* New York: Cambridge University Press, 2001.

Howard E. Williams   *Investigating White Collar Crime: Embezzlement and Financial Fraud.* Springfield, IL: Charles C. Thomas, 2006.

Michael Woodiwiss   *Organized Crime and American Power: A History.* Toronto: University of Toronto Press, 2001.

Index

Global warming, 60, 68
Golden Rule, 98–99
Golem, 66
Goodloe, Charles, Jr., 166
Gorland, Jennifer, 166
Gray, Kenneth R., 92–107
Greed, 100–102, 115, 153, 185, 212
Green, Gary S., 110
Green, Stuart P., 21–39
Greenberg, Hank, 151
Grossen, Cynthia, 130–134
Guilt presumption, 73–74
Gulfstream G450 jet, 113
Gun registration, 27

H

Hamilton, Alexander, 63, 218, 219, 221–222
Hardball negotiating, 27
Harm, definition of, 28–30
Hartmann, Thom, 215–228
Hasnas, John, 31
Health insurance, 15
HealthSouth Corp., 137
Henning, Peter, 152
Henry, Patrick, 220
Hess, Stephen, 251
Higgins, Michael, 177
Hinduism, 99
Hobbes, Thomas, 224
Hochstetler, Andy, 117–129
Hogan, Robert, 87
Hogan Assessment Systems, 87
Hogan Personality Inventory (HPI), 87
Holmes, Sven Erik, 160, 165
Homicide, 29
Hopkinson, Francis, 226
Horning, Amber, 112

HR (Human resources), 86, 89–91
Huinan Tzu, 97
Human resources (HR), 86, 89–91
Human rights, 64
Humane Society, 193
Hynes, Charles, 24

I

Identity theft, 16–17, 19
Illinois, 171
ImClone, 98
Immunity, 43
Impath, 191–192, 197
Incarcerating White-Collar Offenders (Payne), 176
India, 45
Indiana, 165
Indiana University, 131
Indoctrination, 236–238
Indonesia, 59
Industrial Revolution, 219–220
Infidelity, 85, 86–87, 112
Insider trading, 27, 29, 156
Insurance Fraud Bureau of Massachusetts, 174
Integrated Food Technologies, 167
Integrity interviews, 90
Internal Revenue Service, 15, 254
International Business Ethics Institute, 44
International Labor Rights Fund, 59
Internet commerce *See also* Cybercrimes, 214
Internet Fraud Complaint Center (IFCC), 204, 208–209
Investigative Reporters and Editors, 251
Iowa State University, 118